FISHING
THE
NEW JERSEY
COAST

FISHING THE NEW JERSEY COAST

JIM FREDA

BURFORD BOOKS

Printed in the United States of America

10 9 8 7 6 5 4 3 2 1

Library of Congress Cataloging-in-Publication Data

CONTENTS

ACKNOWLEDGMENTS

Writing this book was an extreme pleasure. For one thing it gave me the opportunity to explore the multitude of fishing opportunities that abound in the Garden State. Whether it was banging weakfish under the guardian eye of the Cape May Lighthouse or pulling burly bass from the wave-swept North Jetty of Barnegat Inlet, the experiences gained and memories embraced will be cherished alike. On occasion my wife and three children would accompany me in my travels, which made these long rides that much more enjoyable. The patience and love that my wife demonstrated throughout the writing of this book made it possible. I am forever indebted to her and dedicate this book to her loving ways. I also praise God for His control in all things.

There are many other individuals I would like to thank for their expertise and the time they offered to make this book a reality. These local charter captains, guides, and experts graciously welcomed me to their waters and provided the information that I've passed along to you.

Sincere thanks go out to Captain Dino Torino of Fin Chaser Charters for Sandy Hook Bay, Augie Scafidi for the Navesink River, Captain Bill Hoblitzell for the Shrewsbury River, Captain Dave Chouinard for Spermaceti Cove, Joe Nunziato for the Shrewsbury Rocks, Joe Pallotto for Deal Lake flume, John Scharff for the Shark River, Darin Muly, Shore Catch Guide, for upper Barnegat Bay, Bob Popovics for the North Jetty, Island Beach State Park, Captain Gene Quigley, Shore Catch Charters, for lower Barnegat Bay, Shell E. Caris, Shore Catch Guide, for the South Jetty, Barnegat Inlet, Bruce Hoagland of Bruce and Pat's Bait and Tackle Shop for Long Beach Island, Sean Brennan for Long Beach Island, Scott Albertson of Scott's Bait and Tackle for Graveling Point, Ron Wertz, Bob Hoffman, and Bill Ferris for Brigantine, Captain Bryan DiLeo of Iowa Fortune Guide Service for Ocean City, Captain Joe Hughes, Jersey Cape Guide Service, for Sea Isle City, Jim Mooers of Rod Racks Unlimited for the Wildwoods, Bill Donovan, New Jersey Angler Magazine, for Grassy Sound Channel, and Captain Mark Hansen of the Treemendous charter boat for the Cape May Rips.

Bob Korlishen of Maxmedia Productions, Hoboken, for designing a cover that I feel captures the awesome character of fishing the New Jersey coast. Keith Hamilton of Studio 9 Photography in Waretown for his aerial shot of Long Beach Island that is the cover's watermark.

Fishing buddies John Fields, Captain Frank Bovasso, Captain Brian Pasch, Mickey Alpert, Paul Patruno, and David Goldman for the knowledge I gained while out on the water with them. And Bob D'Amico, Stripersurf.com, for recommending me to Peter my publisher for this work.

I would be remiss if I didn't give special mention to my friends Shell E. Caris and Bob Popovics for the many photos they contributed. The majority of these photos are unique and impressive to say the least. Bob's cover photo of the North Jetty at Barnegat Inlet captures what I feel is a spectacular fishing moment along the New Jersey coast.

INTRODUCTION

When most of us think of New Jersey, the Garden State, images of densely populated cites, suburban sprawl, and miles of parkway and turnpike come to mind. However, our state is much more than just a megametropolis of concrete infrastructure and traffic jams. You can find quaint historical towns and villages, endless farmlands, leaf-laden countrysides, a maze of untouched rivers and streams, and long miles of pristine beaches and wetlands. New Jersey has something to offer to everyone and every sport or recreational activity—if you just know where to look.

Fishing the New Jersey Coast is written with that "where to look" in mind. Where to look for some of the best and most exciting fishing that can be found along the 128 miles of coastline New Jersey has to offer. This book will explore more than 100 of the top-producing locations or hot spots for an angler to hit the suds, cast into a back bay's peaceful and tranquil sunset, wade the tidal flats, or work the inshore waters with a small boat. Whether you're a surf caster, fly rodder, bait fisher, or boater, myriad saltwater fishing possibilities are readily available here in the Garden State.

The fish that I've chosen to discuss in the text are the main targets of the majority of New Jersey anglers: the striped bass, bluefish, weakfish, fluke, winter flounder, and false albacore. These are not, however, the only fish that can be caught from our inshore waters, beaches, or back bays. Many other fish species inhabit our waters that you can target.

The locations that I've chosen are time-proven producers of these selected species and are some of the favorites of local guides, charter captains, and the resident local experts. The text will explore each location, pointing out what species it's best known for, the season or time of year it's most productive, the tactics and tips that will produce fish, and any special considerations you should be aware of.

The text will also expand upon the most popular methods for taking these different species of fish. These will include bait-fishing techniques, plugging or jigging with artificials, fly fishing, and inshore trolling or drifting.

As you read the text, keep in mind that due to the powerful forces of Mother Nature, what you may see one day on the beach can be gone the next. This dynamic characteristic of beaches is responsible for constantly reshaping sandbars, cuts, rips, beach heights, and widths. The honey hole where you hammered fish one day may be completely void of any fish the next. The locations discussed in this text are inevitably at the hands of Mother Nature—and for that matter may have already had their features and topography changed.

On the other hand, man-made changes are also reshaping our beaches here in the Garden State. Beach restoration projects that are currently being conducted by the Army Corps of Engineers are replenishing beaches with sand to provide coastal protection. There are many places along our coastline where homes and businesses meet the water's edge. Devastation to these areas by powerful storms or hurricanes would jeopardize lives and the well-being of many individuals. It would also have far-reaching economic impacts on the tourism industry in this state. This is not to say that the project is without controversy. Many environmental groups and recreational fishermen have voiced strong concerns over loss of habitat and prime fishing locations.

While doing research for *Fishing the New Jersey Coast*, I had the pleasure of meeting, discussing, and fishing the exact locations with the resident charter captains, local guides, and experts. These people helped amass the information presented in this text. Great value is gained from trying fishing tactics and techniques that have deep roots and have withstood the test of time. Keep in mind, however, that the best information you're going to acquire about a specific location will come not only from this book, but also from your own experiences—earned through trial and error and the observations that you make. The real key to your success will be to combine what you learn on the "shoulders of the giants" with your own experiences. Through this process you will become a better angler, because you'll know where all the pieces of the puzzle fit. You will have acquired knowledge with understanding. Good fishin'!

THE NEW JERSEY COAST

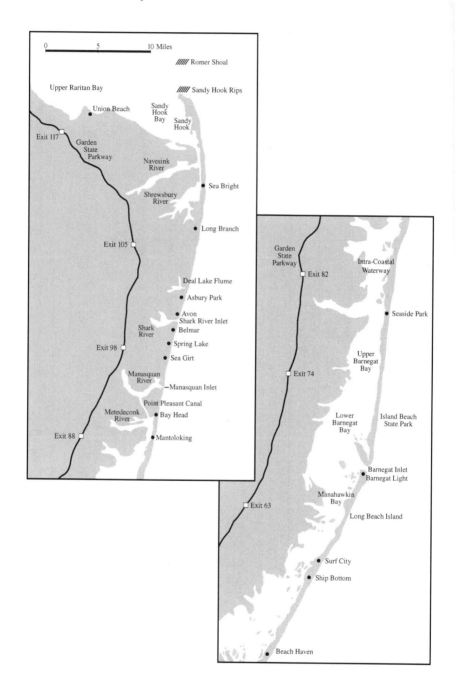

0   5   10 Miles

Romer Shoal

Upper Raritan Bay

Sandy Hook Rips

Union Beach

Sandy
Hook
Bay   Sandy
Hook

Exit 117

Garden
State
Parkway

Navesink
River

Sea Bright

Shrewsbury
River

Long Branch

Exit 105

Garden
State
Parkway

Intra-Coastal
Waterway

Exit 82

Deal Lake Flume

Asbury Park

Seaside Park

Avon
Shark River Inlet
Belmar

Shark
River

Spring Lake

Sea Girt

Upper
Barnegat
Bay

Exit 98

Manasquan
River   Manasquan Inlet

Exit 74

Point Pleasant Canal

Metedeconk
River   Bay Head

Lower
Barnegat
Bay

Island Beach
State Park

Exit 88

Mantoloking

Barnegat Inlet
Barnegat Light

Manahawkin
Bay

Exit 63

Long Beach Island

Surf City

Ship Bottom

Beach Haven

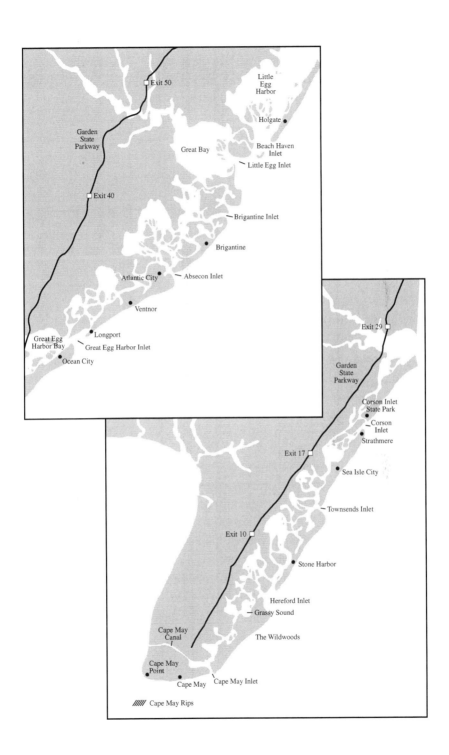

PRIME NEW JERSEY FISHING WATERS
Tip of Sandy Hook

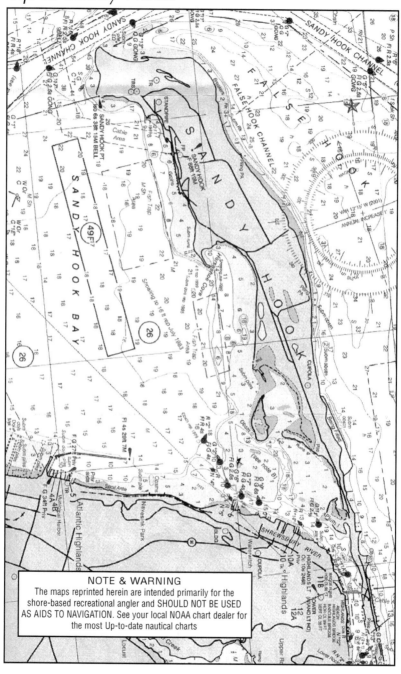

NOTE & WARNING
The maps reprinted herein are intended primarily for the
shore-based recreational angler and SHOULD NOT BE USED
AS AIDS TO NAVIGATION. See your local NOAA chart dealer for
the most Up-to-date nautical charts

Barnegat Inlet

NOTE & WARNING
The maps reprinted herein are intended primarily for the shore-based recreational angler and SHOULD NOT BE USED AS AIDS TO NAVIGATION. See your local NOAA chart dealer for the most Up-to-date nautical charts

Atlantic City/ Absecon Inlet

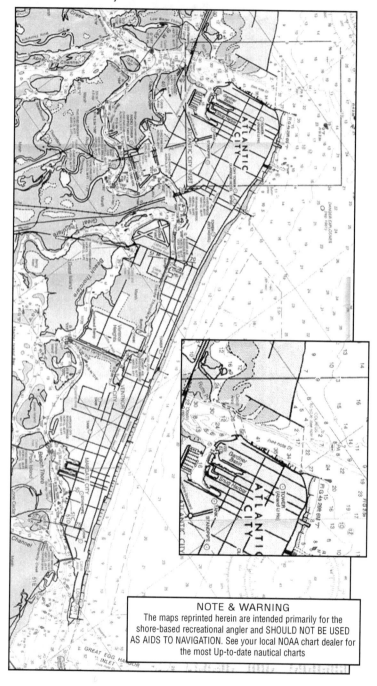

NOTE & WARNING
The maps reprinted herein are intended primarily for the
shore-based recreational angler and SHOULD NOT BE USED
AS AIDS TO NAVIGATION. See your local NOAA chart dealer for
the most Up-to-date nautical charts

Cape May Inlet

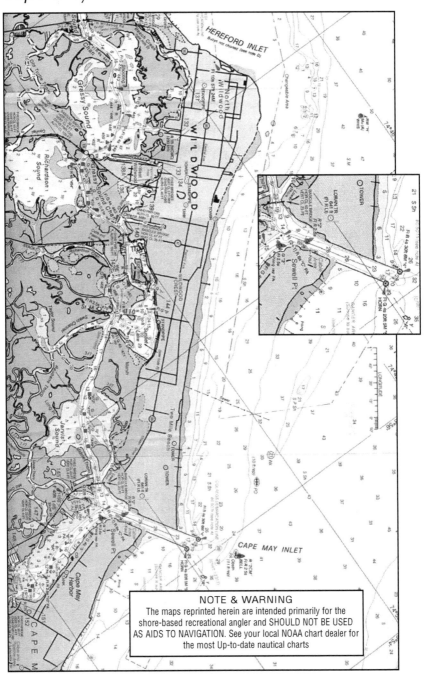

NOTE & WARNING

The maps reprinted herein are intended primarily for the shore-based recreational angler and SHOULD NOT BE USED AS AIDS TO NAVIGATION. See your local NOAA chart dealer for the most Up-to-date nautical charts

ONE

FISH TO CATCH

STRIPED BASS

Without a doubt the striped bass *(Morone saxatilis)* is the most sought-after inshore species along the Jersey coast. This species' cunning ability to perplex even the most experienced angler entices many to pursue it with a passion that borders on obsession. Anglers will stop at almost nothing to lay claim to a trophy linesider. Landing a fish that tips the scales above the 50-pound mark is a quest for many surfsters. Doing so gives you instant credibility and recognition in the fishing community. But there are even bigger bass out there: Commercial fishermen have taken stripers in excess of 100 pounds in the past.

      The striped bass is easily identifiable by the seven or eight stripes that run horizontally along its sides. After it's been in the ocean for a while, the striper takes on a silvery body color with gray and blue tones; in the rivers or bays more brownish tones are exhibited.Stripers range in size along our coast from very small juvenile fish that are found in our back bays to large cows in the 30- and 40-pound range that migrate along our coast in late fall. The International Game Fish Association (IGFA) all-tackle world record is 78 pounds, 8 ounces, caught by Albert

McReynolds on September 21, 1982, from the Vermont Avenue Jetty in Atlantic City.

The striped bass is migratory in nature, preferring a temperature range between 55 and 66 degrees. Bass begin to arrive in our back bay waters in late March; the water there warms quickly after a long cold winter. The largest percentage of the fish that spread out along our coast migrate north from the Chesapeake Bay stock. Many other fish come from Hudson River stock, but these fish usually don't migrate in any great numbers to the southern part of New Jersey. A Delaware Bay stock also adds some significant numbers to our coastal population of bass. It's interesting to note that in the last 10 years more and more fish have begun wintering over in the deeper holes of our estuaries and back bay waters. Many of our tidal rivers—such as the Shrewsbury, Navesink, Manasquan, and Mullica Rivers—have holdover wintering populations. Some have even shown a small natural spawning population. Still, for the most part successful spawns are rare, due to a lack of sufficient current and water depth.

By the time late April and May rolls around the migratory stocks are pretty well dispersed along our coast. During this time the big bass, the spawners, will start to search out freshwater locations to get ready to spawn. The males arrive first, followed by the large females, and finally the smaller females. These fish start to enter freshwater tributaries when the temperature reaches 49 degrees. Spawning will occur when the water temperatures increase to 58 to 64 degrees.

Large females can range well into the 40-pound range, with many females in the 20- and 30-pound class. These fish feed up to the time they spawn, go off their feed when spawning, and then resume feeding when they're spawned out.

In late fall we once again see these migratory stocks moving along our beaches as they return to their wintering grounds. The weeks from Thanksgiving to Christmas are the traditional time for trophy hunting. How close these fish are to the beach is largely dependent on where the bait is moving. If the bait stays offshore, so will the majority of the bass. If the bait is on the beach, the blitz will be on!

BLUEFISH

Along the eastern seaboard bluefish *(Pomatomus saltatrix)* range from Maine to Florida. It's a migratory species, moving northward in spring and southward in fall. Their preferred temperature range is from the upper 50s to high-60-degree range. Thus we see them arriving later in spring and disappearing much earlier in fall from our Jersey waters than the striped bass.

Bluefish are more pelagic in nature than striped bass, and it's therefore much more unpredictable when and where they'll show up along our beaches. They are, however, the mainstay of the party- and charter-boat industry in New Jersey.

Bluefish have greenish, iridescent blue dorsal shading that blends into silver on the sides. The mouth is large, with razor-sharp triangular teeth and a slightly protruding lower jaw. They can get quite large, as indicated by James M. Hussey's IGFA all-tackle record: 31 pounds, 12 ounces, caught January 30, 1972, in Hatteras, North Carolina.

Synonymous with the word *bluefish* we often hear the terms *snapper, cocktail, tailor, slammer* or *alligator*, and *racer* used. These terms are descriptive of a classification by size. A snapper is a juvenile bluefish from several inches to approximately 1/2 pound. A cocktail follows next and ranges up to 2 pounds. A tailor blue is between 2 and 5 pounds. And the slammers or alligators are jumbo blues in excess of 10 pounds. Racers are the hefty blues, 7 pounds or more, that arrive first in our waters in early spring (April and May); they're hungry and fast.

Pound for pound, these yellow-eyed brutes are equal to and in many cases exceed the expectations of even the most experienced angler when it comes to hooking a great sport fish on light tackle. Every blue, no matter how small, will send surges of electrifying energy through your rod that stimulate adrenaline rushes throughout your body.

Bluefish are one of the most vicious and voracious pelagic species to ever inhabit the salty brine. With razor-sharp teeth coupled with elongated, torpedo-shaped bodies and powerfully forked tails, they've evolved into efficient killing machines. So much so that they delight in the act itself, feeding gluttonously until they're full and then regurgitating to feed some more.

Bluefish are ravenous feeders. They have no problem gorging themselves with baitfish.
Bob Popovics photo.

This innate greed makes them an eas target to catch. When blues are on the scene, hooking into them doesn't require artful casting or flawless technique. These predators will devour almost anything that comes across their path. Plugs, jigs, baits, and flies will all catch fish. Using a 4- to 12-inch wire tippet is strongly advisable to prevent the blues from biting through your leader.

WEAKFISH

In the last several years one of the most consistent fisheries along the New Jersey coast has been that for the weakfish. From May to early October an experienced boater can venture to his favorite back bay honey hole and limit out in a very short period of time by jigging bucktails or Fin-S Fish, drifting sandworms, or casting flies. In each of the last several seasons I witnessed and fished weakfish blitzes on the surface that lasted for hours. Many a day there were schools of marauding weaks busting through spearing like ravenous blues, and all well within casting distance of a jetty or beach. The decreased number of bluefish in our waters in recent years has greatly contributed to the rise in our weakfish populations.

Weakfish *(Cynoscion regalis)* are found all along the Atlantic coast, from Cape Cod to Florida. These sea trout—as they are commonly but incorrectly referred to—look a lot like their freshwater brethren, but they're not related. They're actually a member of the drum family and have similarities to croakers.

A weak's body is silvery in appearance with a dark olive or grayish back. Wavy dark lines or dark blotches are distinctive features along the sides and back. The dorsal and tail fins are lightly colored, and the ventral, anal, and marginal fins are yellow. In their mouths are two large canine teeth, but their jaw strength is relatively limited. The soft tissue in their mouths can tear easily when hooked. This is where the fish derives its name, not from its fighting ability. Big weakies are great fighters on light tackle.

Arrivals usually begin at the end of April in Delaware Bay and then progress northward, with good numbers of fish entering central New Jersey at the Manasquan River system by the last week in May. Some of the largest fish of the season arrive early on and can range close to 10 or 15 pounds. These early-spring spawners enter our estuaries and bays searching out suitable spawning beds.

The current IGFA all-tackle world record is 19 pounds, 2 ounces, taken off Jones Beach, Long Island, New York, on October 11, 1984, by Dennis R. Rooney and then matched on May 20, 1989, in Delaware Bay by William E. Thomas. The current New Jersey record is 18 pounds, 8 ounces, caught by Karl Jones in 1986 in Delaware Bay. During the course of an entire season, however, the majority of the fish you hook into will be on the small side, ranging anywhere from 1 to 5 pounds.

John Perrine shows that weakfish are easy and fun to catch. They are a great way to get the youngsters hooked on fishing. Shell E. Caris photo.

Weakfish are attracted to structure and currents, particularly those associated with inlets, canals, river mouths, and tidal creeks. Tidal differences also play a big role in stimulating the fish to feed. Weakfish feed on a wide variety of marine organisms, including grass shrimp, worms, spearing, anchovies, killies, peanut bunker, juvenile herring, baby snappers, spots, croakers, crabs, clams, and other crustaceans.

The incoming tide is the best tide for the shorebound angler to concentrate on. This is particularly true when the incoming tide occurs at night. During the summer months an incoming tide that slacks around midnight is ideal. Not that later isn't productive, but this will allow you to still get home at a somewhat reasonable hour while scoring a good number of fish. With the reduced amount of boat traffic at night, you'll also find weakies to be very aggressive; they can be extremely skittish in the daytime when there's a lot of traffic around.

FALSE ALBACORE

When late September and October rolls around on the Jersey coast we are gladly greeted by some southern guests that come to test our reel drags. Topping the list of these migratory species is the false albacore *(Euthynnus alletteratus)*, aka little tunny, hard tail, or fat albert.

The false albacore has for many reasons replaced the burly linesider in allure, first of all because of its robust fighting ability on light tackle. These pelagic speedsters can quickly strip 200 yards of line in a reel-screeching, arm-wrenching, lightning-fast run. When you add to this the visual component of being able to see your quarry before the strike, your adrenaline will surge to a boil.

Albies can range in size from small football-shaped 3- to 4-pounders up to tuna-looking 15-pounders in New Jersey. The IGFA all-tackle record is 35 pounds, 2 ounces, caught December 14, 1988, by Jean Yves Chatard at Cape de Garde, Algeria.

False albacore are actually a member of the mackerel family and should not be confused with the white albacore tuna that you buy in the grocery store. False albacore have bloodred meat and aren't usually brought to the dinner table.

Albies are one of the most colorful species of fish that you'll catch in New Jersey. Their greenish blue iridescent dorsal surface literally lights up when caught and can be found mixed with hues of sparkling silver and lavender. They possess a deeply forked hard tail and have four to five dark spots located just below the pectoral fins. Series of wormlike vermilion dark lines run across the upper sides of the fish.

Albies feed on a variety of small baits such as spearing, mullet, and peanut bunker, but they have a preference for bay anchovies (rainfish) as they school up along our beaches. Albies have very keen eyesight, so they can be difficult to catch when they're keyed in on a specific bait. For this reason fluorocarbon leaders are usually a must for hooking into these speedsters.

The false albacore has become the prized quarry of the fly fisher in New Jersey. No fish will take you as deep into your backing as quickly as an albie. The window of opportunity for these fish is short, however. Not only will they fly by a beach in literally seconds, but they are also prone to vacate our inshore waters when the surf gets rough or turbid. Albies favor clean, clear water with relatively calm, consistent conditions and plenty of bait to feed on. Preferred temperatures are from the mid-60s to the low-70-degree range. So if we have a cold fall with quickly dropping water temperatures, expect

The false albacore is the prized quarry of the New Jersey fly fisher. Here Bob Popovics displays one of these surf-caught speedsters. Shell E. Caris photo.

the albies to move back south much more quickly.

FLUKE *(Summer Flounder)*

On just about any summer day you'll find small boats, rental boats, and party boats drifting the inshore and back bay waters for fluke *(Paralichthys dentatus)*, also known as summer flounder. The fluke is one of New Jersey's two most common flatfish and is highly sought after when the dog days of summer set in. When fluke are abundant they can litter the seafloor or river bottom and can be "easy pickin's" on the right tide stages. Their meat is white and flaky when cooked and is a favorite dish in many restaurants and homes.

In spring fluke move into our inshore waters from wintering grounds that are located in 400 to 600 feet of water along the edge of the continental shelf. The fluke is a highly predatory fish. This is evident by its large mouth filled with teeth. It's a left-sided fish: The "top" of the fish is actually its left side. This is where you'll find both eyes. The left side of the fish is heavily pigmented, while the right side or belly is white.

The coloration of the fluke varies depending on where the fish is located. Fluke that inhabit muddy bottoms are very dark brown or even blackish in appearance, whereas those inhabiting sandy bottoms are much lighter. Light to dark mottled patterns of spots and blotches will also be evident.

Their average weight is 2 to 6 pounds, but larger "doormats" can be caught ranging from 10 to 20 pounds. The current IGFA record is 22 pounds, 7 ounces, caught by Charles

Shell E. Caris displays a typical New Jersey doormat fluke. Bob Popovics photo.

Nappi on September 15, 1975, off Montauk, New York.

Fluke are aggressive predators and will feed on a variety of baitfish, squid, crabs, and shrimp. They can be caught in our river systems, along the beach, and even offshore in deeper waters. A favorite bait is a killie and squid combo, or sand eels and squid. Strips of fluke belly are also very productive.

WINTER FLOUNDER

After a long cold winter one of the first opportunities that the New Jersey angler has to cure those cabin fever blues comes toward the middle of March when winter flounder *(Pseudo pleuronectes americanus)* season opens. These flatfish are probably among the tastiest fish you can prepare for the table and are highly sought after for this reason, by both the recreational and commercial sectors.

Winter flounder are most abundant in northern and central New Jersey. South of Barnegat Bay their numbers diminish greatly. Winter flounder migrate inshore beginning in October and winter over in our rivers and estuaries. By early December excellent catches are being made.

Winter flounder spawn mostly during January and February, but some early catches in March and April are late spawners and contain plenty of roe. As the water warms again in spring, the fish run offshore.

Morphologically the winter flounder is unusual looking and very similar in appearance to the fluke. It's considered a right-sided fish—in comparison to the left-sided fluke. When you look at the "top" of the fish, you're actually looking at its right side. The winter flounder has a very small mouth and lacks visible teeth. They're usually found lying in muddy or mixtures of muddy and sandy bottoms waiting for small benthic organisms such as worms, snails, and crabs to drift on by for an easy meal. They'll even eat plant material. Their color can vary from a dark brown to gray to olive green with visible dark spots. Their average weight is only 1 to 1 1/2 pounds, but some have reached as large as 5 pounds. The IGFA record is 7 pounds, caught by Einar F. Grell on May 8, 1986, off Fire Island, New York.

Mickey Alpert's quest for that 50 pound surf-caught bass became a reality with this 51.8-pound trophy. Hank Wurzburger photo.

TWO

THE JETTY STATE

New Jersey is well known for its jetty construction. Many of our New Jersey is well known for its jetty construction. Many of our beaches are littered with these rock piles, which were designed to provide coastal protection and prevent beach erosion. The northern and central part of our state has long been referred to as "Jetty Country." The long array of these artificial structures that line towns from Sea Bright through Manasquan have been the playing field for many jetty jocks searching for that trophy catch. But given the state's recent beach replenishment projects, these once prime fishing locations are quickly being covered up or notched. Lucky for us, Mother Nature has her way of undoing what man has done, and many of these jetties are exposed again. You'll also find that many of the improved inlets across the state, such as the Shark River, Manasquan, Barnegat, Absecon, Townsend, Hereford, and Cold Spring, are home to some of the longest and most productive jetties that can be found anywhere.

By definition, a *jetty* is any long artificial structure built perpendicular to the coast to protect the openings of inlets or harbors. A *groin* is a short artificial structure built perpendicular to the shoreline in an effort to control beach erosion by trapping sediments carried by longshore currents. It's common practice to use the term *jetty* to refer to all of the rock structures along our beaches, even though technically this usage is incorrect.

When it comes to fishing the New Jersey coast, jetties make up one of its most productive and challenging components. Fishing these rock piles requires you to always consider safety first and the catch second. Wearing the appropriate footwear, such as steel-studded Korkers, is an absolute must. Without them you're putting yourself at risk for a severe fall or plunge. Since jetties are such a big part of our fishery, a little jetty knowledge may be extremely useful before you begin to tackle these structures.

Jetties provide an avenue for the surf fisherman to hook into fish that would ordinarily be unreachable from the beach. They also provide some excellent structure that holds myriad marine life. These highly productive ecosystems draw bait along their sides, which in turn lures predators. Stripers, blues, weakfish, fluke, and albacore can be found just underneath your Korkers.

Fishing a jetty can be very productive in a northeast blow. Always remember "safety first" during these extreme conditions. Scott Erwin shows how it's done.
Shell E. Caris photo.

Understanding the anatomy of a jetty will help you understand how to fish it productively. Many of the jetties in our state have been constructed so that at mean high tide, they're still 2 feet above sea level and not completely submerged. So even at high tide, they're fishable. A storm or rough surf, however, will render them unsafe, because waves wash over them, sweeping even the most experienced fisherman off his feet.

There are three parts to any jetty: the beach end, the middle section, and the tip. The beach end of the jetty runs all the way back to the zero line, which may be the street, dunes, or a permanent bulkhead. The majority of this portion is covered with sand and never seen by the fisherman. This gives the illusion that the jetty ends where it meets the waterline on the beach. Along the midsection there can be outcroppings of rocks with sheltered covelike features or straight runs of granite rocks. And at the tip you'll find rocks dislodged by strong storms and scattered around on the surrounding sea bottom.

As a fisherman, you'll need to attack the jetty with the same strategy that a trout fisherman uses to attack an unfamiliar stream: that is, to read it. Work its entire length fishing both sides until you learn where the deeper holes and ambush points are located. A good rule of thumb is to fish the tip first, particularly in the early morning at sunup. This is where the largest fish will be located the majority of the time. This makes the tip a rather attractive place, and it can become crowded very quickly, especially if there's easy access and parking available directly behind the jetty on the street.

The tip of the jetty will give you the ability to cast more than 180 degrees. You can fan out and work the rock pile from many different angles. The tip is most favorable at high tide when the water is relatively calm. In rough-water conditions the tip is unfishable due to large waves breaking on top of it or pushing large volumes of white water over the rock face.

Jetties were designed to prevent beach erosion, but in hindsight we now realize that they actually cause more. As the littoral current transports sand along the beach, the jetty acts as a barrier, trapping sand on the side of the jetty that the current is striking. This was the initial purpose of the jetty. It was hoped that this sand would build up and fill in the beach behind the jetty. However, what happens is that the opposite side of the jetty becomes void of any deposition of sand. As a result, a deep hole develops on this side, adjacent to the tip.

This spot is a prime location for trophy fish to be lurking. Spot it quickly and fish it first, before any other anglers have a chance to toss in an offering. Pay particular attention to this spot if the wind is blowing and pushing waves into the hole. This will trap plankton and draw baits into these quarters, making them easy prey. Don't pass up this opportunity when the conditions set up this way. It will be an excellent ambush point with highly productive results.

Once you're comfortable that you've fished the tip exhaustively, you can move to the midsection or beach end of the jetty. The choice is up to you. Both areas are conducive to holding bait and will produce fish. If you move to the midsection, look for outcroppings of rocks along the sides of the jetty. These may be difficult to recognize, because they're sometimes slight and hardly noticeable. Remember that what you see on the surface extends out and continues well below the surface. A small outcropping above will increase in size and length below the water. This is where polarized sunglasses will help; they let you see below the surface by eliminating glare.

One of the most predominant features of the middle section of a jetty is the presence of rip currents, which run along its sides. The edges or tailout sections of rips are excellent places for trophy fish to lie in wait for an easy meal. Along the sides of a jetty, rips will develop as the jetty redirects water moving laterally along the beach. The jetty is an obstacle that the water needs to go around. As a result, deep cuts are carved along the sides of the jetty rocks as the water follows its path of least resistance.

Fishing these rips will undoubtedly put you into fish. To fish the rip from the midsection, cast your line into the beach, allowing it to fall on the backside of an advancing wave. As your line is swept out, let it sink until it's out in front of you at about the one o'clock position. At this point start retrieving slowly, letting the natural flow of water over your plug or fly produce undulations. If you're fly fishing, don't strip too quickly, or your fly will rise to the surface, out of the strike zone.

Another very effective way to fish a rip is to dead drift a weighted jig or fly through it. Cast in the same manner as before, but as your offering is swept out, feed out line also. This will allow your jig or fly to be swept out toward the tail section of the rip without rising to the surface. As your line begins to straighten at the end of the drift, start your retrieve. Be alert for a quick strike as soon as your offering is pulled toward you.

As you move to the beach end of the jetty, you'll usually find a pocket where the beach and jetty meet. This spot warrants close examination, because even large predators frequent it. Don't be fooled into thinking that the shallow water in this area is not a prime fish-holding region. As a matter of fact, it's quite the opposite. Many times predators will trap bait here, using the jetty and the beach as a barrier.

A second beach-end location to work is the beach scarp. This is the region that lies directly in front of you as you enter the water. A drop-off is usually produced from the returning water. This trough serves as an avenue for cruising fish looking for small invertebrates, which are dislodged by the waves' churning action and the returning backwash from the beach slope. Small baitfish also use this area as they follow the topography of the coastline on their migratory routes.

After you work the beach end pocket, fish this trough by casting straight out from your position. Allow the incoming waves to push your line into the trough, then retrieve slowly, directly toward you. If you have a hook-up in this area, you should be able to quickly get off the rocks and onto the beach to fight the fish.

There are some special considerations when fishing a jetty. When retrieving your artificial from any part of the jetty, pull it directly to the edge of the rocks. Allow your offering to sit momentarily in a pocket of water next to the rocks, undulating back and forth. In a last desperate attempt to capture their prey, bass and blues will attack a plug or fly fished in this manner—it appears to be pinned in with no escape.

Special consideration should also be given to fighting a fish from the middle or tip section of the jetty. Hooking any large trophy-sized fish will necessitate getting off the rocks to land the fish, or at least having a predetermined landing route. Walking a fish off the rocks and landing it in the surf is safer than risking having to climb down the rocks and being knocked off the jetty by an unexpected wave. A surf landing is usually possible if you're fishing a short jetty.

A common mistake made by many fishermen after they've successfully walked a fish off the rocks is to immediately begin reeling down on the fish while standing next to the jetty. To eliminate any chance of the fish running back into the rocks, walk a good distance away from them before you begin your retrieve.

As you walk down the beach, let your reel drag and rod bend control the fish while it strips line from the reel. As you apply pressure, try to feel which direction the fish's head is facing, then try to turn the head so it's facing the beach while guiding the fish to swim away from the rocks. Once you're a good distance away from the jetty, you can continue to fight the fish in a normal manner.

If the fish won't allow you to move off the rocks because it's too big or the jetty is too long, look for a flat rock near the water's edge where the fish could be led and slid onto. This will minimize the chances of your leader getting cut on the rocks as you get ready to land the fish. Be ready for one final desperate attempt to escape as the fish realizes the end is near.

And there you have it: some knowledge and strategies to get you started or improve your tactics when confronted with these ominous New Jersey rock piles. Put on the Korkers for safety and play by the rules, and you'll reap the rewards of a trophy fish. And maybe even have bestowed upon you that coveted title . . .jetty jock!

THREE

FLY FISHING

In the last few years the sport of saltwater fly fishing has exploded along the Jersey coast. With the exposure that the sport has received from various sources, such as ESPN Outdoors, numerous Internet sites, and multiple national magazines and publications, more and more anglers are abandoning the heavy hardware and opting for the long rod. Even freshwater fly rodders are coming to the salt, realizing that the sheer size of the quarry will elicit adrenaline rushes that cannot be matched by the feisty 15- and 16-inch salmonids that have been coming to net.

From Sandy Hook to Cape May, myriad opportunities abound for the fly fisherman to do battle with stripers, blues, weaks, and our prized trophy the false albacore. The saltwater long rodder can find an abundance of rock jetties and long stretches of pristine beaches perfectly suited for shooting a line into the suds.

As a saltwater fly-fishing guide, I'm frequently asked, "So why fly?" For me it's the strike and ensuing fight. The sensation of holding a pumping fly rod in your hand is unmatched by any conventional or spinning tackle. The throbbing, pulsating, and bending rod releases its energy directly into your hand.

It's almost as if you have the captured fish by the tail. I like to call it a fly rodder's fix. This is what keeps me returning to the surf time after time, and cast after cast.

There's a fascinating history associated with the sport of saltwater fly fishing in the Northeast. From its New England infancy days in the 1870s to the present, the sport has seen changes spearheaded by several influential and creative individuals. Pioneers such as Zane Grey, Tom Loving, Joe Brooks, Lee Wulff, Holly Hollenbeck, Lefty Kreh, and Stu Apte, to name a few, piloted the sport in its early years, leading to its progression in our seaside communities in the 1960s. At that time two men, Cap Colvin and Fred Schrier, were influential in forming one of the first groups at the Jersey shore that focused on the sport, in 1962. Initial meetings of the Saltwater Flyrodders of America were held at Cap Colvin's Tackle Shop in Seaside Park.

Seven saltwater flies for New Jersey. Top to bottom: Half-and-Half, Siliclone, Surf Candy, Deceiver, Bob's Banger, Clouser, Jiggy. Pete DeStefano photo.

With men like Cap Colvin, Lefty Kreh, Mark Sosin, Frank Woolner, Vin Sparano, Lou Rhodia, Butch Colvin, and Eddie Morrison, a new era of catching fish along our New Jersey beaches had emerged, with new techniques and strategies. This initial surge to establish the sport in our area carried a punch that lasted into the early 1970s, but by the latter part of the decade the flame had been diminished.

By the mid-1980s saltwater fly fishing once again saw a resurgence along the Jersey shore. The impetus was one of the most influential and innovative saltwater fly tiers known today, Bob Popovics. Bob assembled a noteworthy group of fly fishers—Don Wall, Doc Fort, Fred Schrier, Tom Fote, Eddie Morrison, Lance Erwin, Ed Jaworowski, Hank Brandenburg, Joe Patton, Dick Dennis, Bill Hoblitzell, Marie DeSaules, and Joe Cavanaugh—and the flame was rekindled. With these men and women Bob went on to establish what is today New Jersey's largest saltwater fly-fishing club, the Atlantic Saltwater Flyrodders, based out of Seaside Park.

To get started in this sport with moderately priced gear from a reputable manufacturer will cost in the neighborhood of $400 to $500. In this price range your rod and reel will have a lifetime warranty. If either breaks, the manufacturer will handle the repair or replacement. If this price is too steep for your budget, the major mail-order fishing catalogs and sports stores offer starter outfits that run in the neighborhood of $200. The workmanship and quality, however, will not be the same.

If you're a beginner to the sport, look to purchase a 9-foot 9- or 10-weight rod. It should have a medium-fast action with a progressive taper—also referred to as a midflex rod. This rod will load through the upper half of the blank, which offers more of a feel for what's meant by *loading the rod*. A fast-action rod that loads more in the tip section will not deliver as much rod flex and will be difficult for a beginner to handle.

Your choices in reels are equal in number to the rod selections on the market today. You'll want to purchase a high-end, direct-drive, disc-drag reel. Trying to hit the suds with a pawl-type drag (found on some trout reels) just won't cut it if a trophy fish comes your way.

I favor a large-arbor reel, because when fully loaded with backing its increased spool diameter allows for more line pickup with each wind. If a nice-sized fish is running toward you, taking up line quickly is going to be important. The majority of the fish you catch along the Jersey coast will not take you deep into your backing—but a teen-sized bass or false albacore definitely will.

There are a number of different types of fly lines of various designs, tapers, and sink rates. Floating, slow-sinking, and fast-sinking lines or heads are available. The easiest line for a beginner to cast is a full-length weight-forward floating line. Match the line weight to your rod's weight. Your workhorse line, however, will be a full-length weight-forward intermediate line. This line will sink at the rate of 1 1/2 to 2 inches per second, allowing you to stay in better contact with the fly upon retrieval. It will also let you cover more water in a vertical plane. Sinking lines, 250 to 850 grains, have sink rates that range from 5 to 12 inches per second and are much more difficult for a beginner to lift out of the water. Their overall weight also makes casting much more difficult.

As a beginner, you'll be better off avoiding a shooting-head system until you've learned the fundamentals of good casting. These systems do give you more distance, but they collapse on a beginner as soon as the head is extended out beyond the rod tip.

A general rule to follow when hitting the suds is that if the water is clear and calm, you'll need a longer leader; if it's rough and discolored, you can get away with a shorter one. For beginners, longer leaders should fall in the 7- to 8-foot range. Shorter leaders should be in the 3- to 5-foot range. Short leaders can be a straight section of 15- or 20-pound monofilament looped directly to the end of the fly line.

If you use a longer leader, you'll need to taper it. This will help the leader turn over rather than falling straight down into a pile at the end of your cast. The tapered leader will continue to transmit energy from the fly line.

To construct your tapered leader, begin by using a nail knot or Albright knot to connect a 6-inch piece of 40- to 60-pound hard mono to the fly line. At the other end, tie a surgeon's loop. This short section will help turn over the leader. From here use a loop-to-loop connection to attach the butt section of your leader. It can be 2 feet of 25-pound test. Blood-knot this to a 2-

foot section of 20-pound test, followed by another blood knot to end with 15-pound mono or fluorocarbon. You can reduce the number of leader sections to two as the total length of your leader is shortened to about 5 feet. Use a trilene or improved clinch knot to attach all your flies that don't have lead heads or lead eyes (like you find on Jiggy Flies and Clousers). Attach these with a loop knot.

The easiest flies for the beginner to cast are Deceiver patterns 3 to 4 inches long. Begin with basic colors: olive/chartreuse and white, blue and white, all-white, yellow, or black. Look for the following seven flies to cover most of the baits that you encounter in New Jersey: Lefty's Deceivers, Clouser Minnows, Half-and-Halfs, and Bob Popovics's Jiggies, Surf Candies, Bangers, and Siliclones.

A piece of equipment that you won't want to be without is a stripping basket. In most instances the stripping basket can be considered the fly fisherman's best friend. This basket is designed to hold your fly line upon retrieval. Stripping line into the basket will prevent it from falling into the surf wash or jetty rocks.

If most of your fishing is going to be in the surf, make sure you wear a basket that has drainage holes in it. This way any wave splash will easily flow out of the basket. If you're going to be mostly wading in back bays, opt for a basket with no holes, which will allow you to wade out as far as possible; the basket floats on top of the water, and no water enters it (which would lift the line out of the basket and float it away).

These are the basics you'll need to get started. Include a gear bag loaded with all the accessories, look for good conditions, calm surf, and light winds, put on the Korkers for safety, and you're ready to go.

FOUR

LOCATIONS

UPPER RARITAN BAY
PEBBLE AND UNION BEACH

The saltwater fishing season for most New Jersey anglers begins around the second week of March. All over the state anglers begin to move to the back bay waters and estuaries in search of the state's most sought-after species—the striped bass. The striper is the first fish to arrive on the scene that can truly put a bend in the rod. The extensive back bay systems in New Jersey have become a wintering ground for a resident population of local bass. These fish are considered shorts and will become active once the water temperature begins to rise above 45 degrees.

By the middle of March our back bay waters have begun to warm as their shallow, muddy bottoms absorb the rays from the increasing amount of sunlight. In addition, warm-water runoff from early-spring rains raises the bay's temperature quickly and inputs organic nutrients that stimulate the productivity of the natural food chain for another season. Stripers will come right into the shoreline's warm waters as they begin to scour the bottom for any tasty morsel.

A favorite early-season striper spot for many Monmouth County anglers is Pebble and Union Beach, located on the south shore of Raritan Bay.

Raritan Bay is part of the Port of New York and New Jersey's marine estuary system. It's charted as part of the New York Bight, which includes New York Harbor's Lower Bay, Jamaica Bay, Sandy Hook Bay, and the immediate Atlantic Ocean coastal waters. Its name comes from the Naraticong Indian tribe of the Raritang Nation, which once used these waters.

The bayshore beaches extend for a distance of approximately 11 miles from Pebble Beach to False Hook at the mouth of Sandy Hook Bay. Areas to the north of Pebble Beach are also very productive in early spring. Both locations have many areas that can be fished from shore or by kayak. These areas are also accessible by boat from any of the many boat launches in the area. The Leonardo State Marina, in Middletown Township, has a free public launch ramp and facilities; in Keansburg you'll find a fishing pier that juts out well into the bay.

The earliest striper action that takes place at Pebble and Union Beach is on bloodworms fished by the dead-stick method on high-low rigs. This two-hook rig will place your baits on and just off the bottom, putting them in a striper's direct view. Not much weight is needed to hold the bottom, because the currents in this area aren't strong; 1/2 to 1 1/2 ounces of lead will be sufficient.

Pebble Beach is also an excellent area for fly rodders to hook into some early-season bass, particularly when the water warms into the mid-50s. There are three locations that traditionally produce fish that need to be shared between the bait fishermen and the fly guys. When you reach the bay, bait fishermen set up in the area immediately out in front. Trying to use a fly rod along these sod banks isn't practical. Instead, fly fishers can walk east along the bank to the first point. There you'll find a small creek with a good-sized sandbar at its mouth that you can wade onto. During a falling tide you can wade out a good distance from shore. It's a good idea to fish as you wade out. Don't overlook the shallow water directly in front of you. If you don't get any hits, wade out to waist-deep water and fish the drop-off at the edge of the bar.

The second location for the fly rodder is found about 400 yards to the left of the access point as you enter the bay. If you walk completely around the bowl on your left, you'll find another wadable sandbar. The bar is visible at low tide, and it'll take you a good distance out from shore.

One of the advantages of fly fishing in the bay is that its relatively shallow depth allows you to position yourself so that the wind is always at your back. In other words, while you're wading away from the shore you can maneuver 360 degrees and always have fishable water in front of you. Many times you'll have fish busting right in front of you that are otherwise well out of reach of the shorebound angler.

The bay is a great place for someone just getting into saltwater fly fishing to learn. You don't have to deal with the rough surf conditions, stronger winds, and rip currents found along the outer beaches. Lighter rods, such as 8- and 9-weights, will work just fine, because most of the fish will be smaller than you encounter on the beach. Clousers, Jiggy Flies, Deceivers, or Half-and-Halfs fished on intermediate- or slow-sinking lines will consistently produce fish.

The exception to this, however, is when the big bunker come into spawn—usually during the second or third week of April. These adult bunker attract some really big bass that can tip the scales in the 20- or 30-pound range. This is when you'll want to switch over to an 11-weight rod and throw large Doll Eye bunker patterns. Bait fishermen can score with bunker chunks or bunker heads fished on short-shank 6/0 or 7/0 hooks.

Once May rolls around the bay will be invaded by bluefish. For the fly rodder it's time to break out the trace wire tippets to keep your flies from being bitten off. Poppers or Bob Popovics's Bangers will produce very well.

Another interesting phenomenon that occurs toward the end of May and the beginning of June is a cinderworm hatch. This event usually coincides with high tide during the new-moon phase of the month. These worms are 1 to 4 inches in length and reddish brown in appearance. They swim erratically near the surface as they enact their spawning ritual. Bass love these tiny marine annelids and can become very selective and difficult to catch on this feed. Your best bet is to drift small cinderworm patterns tied with chenille bodies and marabou tails. The marabou provides a movement that nicely simulates the worm's erratic behavior and elicits strikes. Don't be afraid to tie on a second similar fly as a dropper.

As late fall arrives along the bayshore, anglers have another excellent opportunity to hook into quality-sized bass. The juvenile bunker, better known as peanut bunker, that were maturing over the summer are now ready to make their move south along the coast. By the time late October and early November rolls around, these peanut bunker average 3 to 5 inches long.

Peanut bunker are silvery with white bellies and have a single black spot under the pectoral fin. Their profile has length and height but lacks width. Their length is 2 to 5 inches (or longer), depending on age; their flanks are about 1 inch high; viewed from below, their width is minimal.

Both fly rodders and bait fishermen can score heavily at this time. For fly rodders, peanut bunker patterns such as Geno's Baby Angel, Slab Flies, or bulky white Deceivers will produce best. If you're spin fishing, you'll have the best results if you live-line a peanut bunker.

LIVE-LINING

To live-line a baby bunker, you'll first need to obtain your baits by either netting them or snagging them. To net your baits, you'll need a 5- to 6-foot-diameter cast net and some skill in throwing the net into the pods as they move along the beach. If the cast net is too cumbersome for you to use you can opt for a second method: snagging a peanut bunker with a homemade snag rig. Place a 3/4 to 1 1/2-ounce egg sinker on your main running line, then attach the line to a 75-pound-sized barrel swivel. A 24- to 36-inch leader of 20- to 30-pound test is then attached to the barrel swivel and a 1/0 treble hook tied to the other end. If you're going to fish the peanut on the snag rig, use a bronze treble hook so that if your fish breaks off the hooks will just rust out.

Most anglers, however, transfer the peanut to a second rod with a size 2/0 to 4/0 Gamakatsu live-bait hook on it. This is placed just above the dorsal. You don't need any terminal tackle or weight. Cast the bait into the school and let it go. Get ready for a quick take. Bass have a cunning ability to pick out the weak or wounded of the bunch.

If you choose to use artificials, the hardware that will be most effective is on the small side, with a wide profile. Swimming plugs such as small Danny or custom wood swimmers are always effective, as are 1/2- to 3/4-ounce Rat-L-Traps because of their wide body. For poppers, the 1-ounce Gibbs Polaris popper is my number one choice. The Atom Proppa popper and Striper Swiper in 3/8 to 7/8 ounce are also good. In soft plastics, 4-inch shad bodies are slightly favored over Fin-S Fish, but both will produce. For all these artificials, white or pearl is the preferred color.

If you're tossing metal, the Hopkins Shorty, 1-ounce Kastmaster, 3/4- to 1-ounce Krocodile, 1 1/2-ounce Luhr Jensen Cast Champ, and 2-ounce crippled herring are the ones to use. Allow them to fall through the school; flutter when you retrieve, rather than moving them along the same line. This will imitate an injured bait. Don't overlook that old standby, the white bucktail jig, either. Jigging one near the bottom is usually deadly.

To get to Pebble and Union Beach, take the Garden State Parkway to exit 117 and head east on Route 36. Go to the fourth light and make a left onto Poole Avenue. Go through the first light to the next stop sign. If you make a right onto Florence Avenue and go to the end of the road, this is Union Beach. If you take the left fork at the stop sign and head straight to the end of the road (1.1 miles), you're at Pebble Beach. There's a dirt lot on the left where you can park. At Pebble Beach you'll need to park and walk 1/4 mile along a dirt path to reach the sod banks along the shoreline. At Union Beach you can park along the street; the beach is directly out in front.

SANDY HOOK

NORTH BEACH/FALSE HOOK

The northernmost part of the New Jersey coastline begins at Sandy Hook. This 7-mile-long, 1,665-acre barrier spit is surrounded by water on three sides and has actually been completly separated from the mainland as an island many times in the last several hundred years. Because of its strategic location, Sandy Hook has deep historical roots in our nation's military archives. Lying at the entrance to New York Harbor, Sandy Hook has played a crucial role in defending and protecting this waterway for more than two centuries.

The historic Sandy Hook Lighthouse (originally called the New York Light) was built in 1764 and served as a beacon for navigating entrance to the harbor. Originally the light stood 500 feet from the tip of the hook, but today it's nearly 1 1/2 miles from the northernmost tip. The northern migration of the hook's tip is due to the littoral transport of sand along the beach. This littoral flow is from south to north and has caused the hook to curve and change topographically over the last 10,000 years. New hooks have formed and left old ones behind. This is evident when you look at both Spermaceti and Horseshoe Coves; both mark spots where the hook ended in the past. Periodic dredging is still necessary today to keep the shipping channel in Sandy Hook Bay open.

The extensive array of salt marshes, coastal habitats, maritime holly forest, and history found so close the metropolis has made Sandy Hook one of the most popular vacation spots along the Jersey coast. Because four major river systems (Hudson, Raritan, Shrewsbury, and Navesink) feed the bay, the area is also well known for drawing fishermen from surrounding states.

Today Sandy Hook is part of the Gateway National Recreation Area, maintained by the National Park Service, Department of the Interior. It's one of the more than 360 parks that comprise the system. It's also a site on the New Jersey Coastal Heritage Trail.

As you enter Sandy Hook at the toll plaza, you're on the area of the peninsula known as the critical zone. This area has been completely submerged many times during large nor'easters, effectively cutting off the hook from the mainland. There's good fishing in this area, on both the ocean side and the bay side. The mouth of the Shrewsbury River is located at this point on the bay side, and this is always a good location to fish. There's good access to this area along the banks of Plum Island.

The Highlands Bridge, directly across from the entrance to Sandy Hook, offers access under its abutments on either side of the river but calls for special tackle and techniques due to the strong currents that flow around it. Most of the fishing in this area requires 60- to 80-pound braid loaded on conventional reels and stiff rods. You'll need heavy bucktail ball jigs with size 6/0 to 8/0 hooks to get you down when the tide is ripping. Large bass can be caught from these waters, and this tackle will give you the necessary power and leverage to keep the fish from heading down into the rubble and breaking you off. You'll also notice many anglers fishing from the top of this bridge at night. Most of the time this isn't permitted and is regulated by the bridge tender or municipal police.

Our main area of focus, however, is North Beach, located at the northernmost end of the hook. If I had to pick one spot to fish on the hook, this is it. To get to North Beach, follow the roadway beyond the toll plaza for approximately 4 miles. You'll see signs for North Beach and the parking area. A large observation deck here gives a breathtaking view of the New York skyline. As you walk onto the beach, you'll spot a small jetty that's a good spot to begin your fishing. Work the tip of this jetty with plugs or flies, looking for any cuts or troughs behind a shallow sandbar that can set up at this point. Looking northward approximately 1/3 mile, you'll see what looks to be the tip of Sandy Hook. This is False Hook; the actual tip is located around this point 2 miles to the west, where the Coast Guard station is located. The False Hook is actually a submerged shoal that sits just beyond The False Hook Channel off the beach.

This stretch of water along the shoreline is well worth

investigating. You'll find all the species of fish in this area, but it's best known for its excellent striper and bluefishing. Many times throughout the year blitz conditions will result as the bait stacks up. This occurs more frequently here than at any other spot along the central New Jersey coast. This is one of the reasons why North Beach has such an excellent reputation.

As you walk toward The False Hook, the inside edge of False Hook Channel is within casting distance. The deeper water along this shoreline usually keeps wave heights to a minimum. On rough days when there are good breakers along the beaches to the south of the hook this area can be surprisingly flat. The curving of the hook toward the mainland at this point also helps prevent this area from getting a direct hit.

As you walk to the point of The False Hook, keep an eye out for any activity on the water's surface that would be a telltale sign of the presence of fish. If you see swirls, for instance, or bait being pushed to the surface, stop and take a cast. Sometimes you'll note much more subtle changes, such as a slick on the surface or a keen-eyed tern circling over a particular spot.

When you get to the tip of The False Hook, you've reached the mouth of Sandy Hook Bay. This area is extremely productive because of the currents and rips that form along the point. These rips are located within casting distance and should be fished by allowing your bait, plug, or fly to drift through them at different depths. The rips continue along the beach as you walk west around the point. Many different methods are used along this shoreline. The rip extends on the inside along the beach up to the point where the shoreline begins to bowl inward. The inside of The False Hook also offers shelter from the wind when it's blowing hard from the south or southeast. You'll be able to fish here, nicely tucked behind the sand dunes, when the ocean side may be unfishable.

The beach along the inside of the hook is also an ideal place for the fly fisherman to shoot some casts. There are no waves to contend with, and the rip allows for long unimpeded drifts. Bulkier-profile flies tied with feathers and saddle hackles in white produce well, because they mimic some of the larger baits—especially bunker and herring—that are present during the season. When held in the current, these imitations will undulate back and forth, drawing strikes. Be ready with wire tippets, however, because the blues that invade this area will really do a number on your flies.

Drifting the area around The False Hook in a small boat is a sure way to hook into quality-sized fish. Close to shore the water is 10 to 15 feet deep just inside the main channel; the channel drops off into the 20-foot range. The currents that rip through here can be treacherous at times, particularly in a wind-against-tide situation, so a small-boater will need to exercise caution. Also, the large charter-boat fleet uses this channel to get to the waters along the oceanfront. These 60-footers throw a wake that can easily put you in trouble.

If you're fishing for stripers or blues, experiment with drifting your baits or artificials at different levels in the water column. Look for surface-feeding action and working birds as an indicator that the fish and bait are up in the water column. If you're targeting weakfish or fluke, use enough weight or a heavy enough jig to bounce the bottom. This will vary depending on the current and tidal flow.

Night fishing in this area is also extremely popular because of the sensational view of the New York skyline. It's a rather spectacular site to be fishing, with such a breathtaking view in the distance. You'll need a parking permit, however, to remain on the hook at night. This can be obtained for a fee from the ranger station just beyond Spermaceti Cove and is good for an entire year.

Parking at the hook is permitted in designated areas and requires a fee that's in effect 7 A.M. to 4 P.M. from Memorial Day through Labor Day. There's no fee at other times of the year. Roadside parking is not permitted.

To get to Sandy Hook, take Route 36 east to its end; you're there. Or head north along Ocean Avenue through the towns of Monmouth Beach and Sea Bright until you get to the entrance to the hook.

SANDY HOOK
THE RIP/BUG LIGHT

At the tip of Sandy Hook is a spot well known throughout the state as the Rip. The Sandy Hook Rip has been highly publicized for the trophy fish that can be taken from its waters. It's located at the true end of the Hook, where Sandy Hook Bay begins to empty into the Atlantic Ocean. The Rip runs very close to the shoreline, so you can access it either by boat or on foot.

The strong currents here are due to a combination of tidal changes, wind direction, and the refraction of water around the Hook's tip. If the wind is against the tide, you can expect some rather treacherous going in a small boat. Breakers will form, and it's easy for a small boat to capsize if it gets turned the wrong way.

As you make your way out to the tip of Sandy Hook by boat, you'll see the historic Fort Hancock and its gun batteries, built to protect the harbor and New York City from attack by sea. The fort was named for Civil War general Winfield Scott Hancock in 1895. You'll also see the Coast Guard station and Bug Light on your right.

Piercing through the dunes in the background is the Sandy Hook Lighthouse, originally known as the New York Light. Built in 1764, this is the nation's oldest operating lighthouse. When it was constructed it stood just 500 feet from the tip of the hook; today it sits 1 1/2 miles back, due to sand deposition at the hook's end.

You'll find that fishing the Rip from the beach is very productive for any of the species of fish mentioned in this text—though the real lure here is striped bass. Getting to the Rip, however, isn't easy. You need to walk a well-marked soft sand trail over the dunes for about 3/4 mile. I recommend traveling light and either carrying your waders or wearing breathables. Also, have a plan if you're considering taking home your catch; tail-dragging a keeper-sized bass can be burdensome.

When you reach the beach from the sand trail, you'll need to continue on foot along the shoreline for another 1/2 mile. Turn left and walk beyond the first point that you see. From here on you'll see the Rip running very close to the beach. You can wade out into the water and cast—but be careful of passing vessels, which throw rather large wakes. You can reach the waters of the Rip with spinning or conventional gear. With a fly rod you'll need the wind at your back to cast to its outer edge.

You can continue to walk around the tip of the Hook toward the Bug Light. The water refracts nicely around this point, and there's a good current. This entire area can be explosive with its plentiful bait. In summer small blues are almost always present and will put a nice bend in your rod.

As you head out to the Rip by boat via the Shrewsbury or Navesink River, look for historic Twin Lights of the Highlands gazing over your shoulder as you pass under the Highlands Bridge. Stay in the channel; there are sandbars on either side of it. After the last buoy, located near the end of Horseshoe Cove, it's pretty much wide open, and the threat of running aground on a sandbar is limited. Here you'll encounter the baymen—Sandy Hook clammers—as they painstakingly rake the bottom for clams.

This 37- pound trophy bass was caught by Tim Burden in the middle of the day. Jim Freda photo.

When you reach the Bug Light at the Coast Guard station, you've made it to the tip of the Hook. This is approximately 8.2 miles from the Highlands Bridge by way of the channel. Here you'll see numerous large party boats out of the Atlantic Highlands and New York drifting these waters for fluke. This is indeed a great location to drift for flatties, due to the irregular topography of the bottom coupled with quick drop-offs.

The drift around the Hook will put you in 25 feet for the most part, but you'll find one hole that drops off to 44 feet and another that drops to 70 feet. These holes are located within several hundred yards of the beach.

As you move farther east, the channel remains deep very close to the beach. It drops to 20 feet just on the beach side of the channel and then to 40 feet within the channel. Here you'll see numerous fishermen who've taken the arduous walk across the dunes to get to the Rip. The distance from this point to The False Hook is 2 miles.

The majority of the boaters who fish the Rip are after striped bass. Peak activity comes in May and June as the bass follow the large schools of bunker that have entered the bay to spawn. April can also offer good action; this is when bunker are traditionally first sighted entering the bay. The summer months of July and August offer good nighttime fishing in the deeper sections of the Rip.

The majority of the boaters will be bunker chunking. Heads and midsections of the bunker produce best. The trick is to use a large chunk with a large enough hook—size 6/0 to 7/0—if you're after the large bass that roam in these waters. Indeed, the bass at the Rip are some of the largest in the state. Teen-and 20-pound stripers are common, along with a good number of 30-pounders. This area also produces a decent number of 40-pound fish during the season, and even some 50-pounders.

If you're going to release your fish, I recommend using a circle hook, which will result in fewer gut-hooked fish. The abundance of short stripers here means using a treble hook is definitely not advisable. These hooks will do considerable damage to the inside of a small striper's mouth.

CHUNKING

Your drift will dictate how much weight you'll need to get your bait into the strike zone. During slack tides and slow drifts you can chunk without any weight at all; chunks will naturally float to the bottom. The rig preferred by most chunkers is a 7- to 8-foot conventional rod loaded with 20- or 30-pound test; short-shank, wide-gap hooks from 5/0 to 7/0; and either a fishfinder rig or three-way swivel to attach the appropriate amount of lead to the leader. Use enough weight to get to the bottom, or just enough so that the chunk drifts along the bottom with the current.

Getting fresh bunker is one of the keys to having a great day. These can either be snagged or netted if you come up upon a tightly packed school. Frozen bunker will catch fish, but not with the same degree of success you'll experience with fresh oily bait. If the bunker are large, you can cut four to five chunks from one bait. Toss a few chunks into the water to create a chum slick to get the bass's attention, but don't overdo it—you want the bass to take the bait, not sit there and have a free meal.

When a bass takes the chunk it will do so with authority. In other words, it will inhale it in one swoop. Give the bass some slack in the line as it runs from the boat, and then lean back on your rod with considerable force to set the hook. Don't be gentle or shy; it will take all the muscle you have to drive the hook home into the hard bony palate of a large bass. Sharpening your hooks to a fine point will definitely give you an advantage. The longer you wait before the strike, the greater the chance that the bass will be gut-hooked.

To get to the Rip by boat you can use any of the launch ramps located at the marinas along the Ocean Avenue side of the Shrewsbury River or the Atlantic Highlands side off Bay Avenue. The other alternative is to use the Atlantic Highlands Marina municipal ramp. This is found at First Avenue and Simon Lake Drive off Route 36 as you head west away from the hook.

If you're going to fish the Rip on foot, drive to the end of the roadway at the entrance to Fort Hancock, where the road forks. Bear left and travel along "Officer's Row" until you get to the Coast Guard station. Make a right onto Canfield Road, then take your first left. At the end of this road make another left and pull into the gravel parking lot. You'll see the abandoned bunkers of Nine Gun Battery directly in front of you. Park toward the end and walk the fisherman's trail along the dunes to the Rip. The trail is posted and easy to follow, even in the dark. If you venture off the trail, you'll be in a restricted wildlife area for nesting birds. You'll also have a nice encounter with one of Sandy Hook's most abundant types of vegetation, poison ivy.

SANDY HOOK
HORSESHOE COVE

As you drive out to the end of Sandy Hook via the main road, you'll see the Shrewsbury River on your left. The river empties into Sandy Hook Bay just north of the Highlands Bridge. From the bridge the road runs for 3.5 miles to the entrance to historic Fort Hancock; you'll see the Nike missile display directly in front of you. Just before this location you'll see Horseshoe Cove on your left and a small parking area on your right. You can identify the spot by a wooden footbridge that runs across the entrance to the wildlife management area salt marsh.

Horseshoe Cove is well worth investigating, either by boat or by wading. Early in the season—April and May—good concentrations of herring and spearing enter these waters, drawing in some nice stripers. In summer the area produces good catches of fluke. Boaters should exercise caution, however, because sand spits have formed around the cove, making it easy to run aground. There are also sunken pilings close to the point near the old artillery bunker.

The area has a rich history. Hundreds of years ago Horseshoe Cove was the end of Sandy Hook, but northerly drifting sands due to the littoral current have changed that significantly today. During the 1500s the first Europeans to set foot in this area were crew members from the *Half Moon,* commanded by Henry Hudson. As early as the Revolutionary War, Sandy Hook served as a strategic military stronghold to protect the entrance to the New York Harbor. British loyalists defended it to ensure British access to New York City.

The U.S. Army first occupied the area during the War of 1812—an occupation that continued through the Civil War, World War I, and World War II. The army later created a proving grounds for new artillery at Sandy Hook. In the 1950s Nike Air Defense Missiles were added. As you explore the northern end of the hook, you'll see the remains of the artillery and mortar batteries once occupied by our armed forces.

During the early part of the spring season Horseshoe Cove can offer excellent fishing for striped bass, weakfish, and bluefish. Since the cove is located just beyond the mouth of the Shrewsbury River, its waters warm much more quickly than the ocean. This is due to the runoff from the warm spring rains that are pumped in by the river. The shallow darker muddy bottom also absorbs the sun's rays, adding considerably to the warming effect. It's not uncommon to find surf temperatures on the ocean side struggling to hit 50 degrees while the cove is registering water temperatures of 57 or 58 degrees.

Another saving grace that this area has to offer is shelter from the wind. Even when the wind is blowing hard from the northeast or southeast on the ocean, you'll find calm conditions on either side of the Cove point. It's a valuable option that can mean a fishing trip to the Hook is not lost in high winds.

There are several areas worth fishing when you wade the points in the Cove. Before you start to walk out across the footbridge, notice the rock jetty wall directly to your left. This area parallels the main road and is a good spot to sit and relax while fishing blood- or sandworms in the early season. There isn't much room to backcast here, however, so plugging or fly fishing is not a good choice.

Once you cross over the footbridge you can walk along the Cove's banks. This entire area is fishable and holds both bait- and gamefish. Walk out to the first point and work the area in front of you. If it's low tide you can wade into the water for a considerable distance. Work your casts so as to cover all the water around you. Don't hesitate to cast back toward the beach and work the water behind. Many fish have been taken by this method.

You can fish a wide variety of artificials or live baits to hook into stripers, bluefish, weakfish, fluke, or winter flounder. You can cover a lot of ground while fishing bucktail jigs or soft-bodied Fin-S Fish for stripers, or an assortment of plugs such as Bombers, Megabaits, Yozuris, and Rebels. The plugs grow more effective as the water warms into the upper 50s. For summer fluke the traditional killie and squid strips or sand eels work well.

In early spring, when huge bunker schools are present in the bay, hooks baited with bunker or mackerel chunks will produce some of the largest bass. Bloodworms will produce good, consistent numbers of short bass.

Fly fishers will find this area very conducive to casting. There are no obstructions to impede either your forward or your backcast. The timing of the tide will dictate what type of sink rate you should use. For the most part, in early spring a Teeny 250 sinking line will work well. This line will slowly sink to the bottom without getting hung up, whereas a Teeny 350 or higher often results in snagging the bottom. This line will bring your flies into the strike zone near the bottom where the fish are milling around during the early part of the season.

As late spring and summer approach, an intermediate line works well. This line sinks at a rate of 1 1/2 to 2 inches per second and will cover the water column from top to bottom. At this time of year fish will be distributed throughout the water column from top to bottom, and surface activity will occur frequently. When the bluefish arrive, you may want to switch to a floating line and use surface poppers to draw their attention.

Once you finish fishing this first point, look north to see the remains of one of the old artillery bunkers. This bunker is at the farthest point of the cove. If it's low tide, you can walk along the shoreline to this point; there's a path that will take you in front of the bunker. If the tide is high, you'll need to access this point from the backside. This can be done from a trail behind the bunker, or from the roadway where you parked your vehicle. Instead of walking across the footbridge, walk north along the roadway past the restricted salt marsh on your left. At the end of the marsh you'll see a nice beach, which will lead you directly to the point of this bunker. These backside waters are worth checking out and will put you in a perfect location when the wind is blowing hard out of the south or southeast. The elevated dune behind you nicely blocks the wind.

When you get to the bunker point, you'll need to be careful as you walk along the concrete rubble. For the most part it's flat here, however, and no more hazardous than walking on a jetty. Some nice flat rocks that extend out on this point provide a good casting platform to reach well out into the bay. Any of the fish mentioned in this text can be caught from this point at the appropriate season.

Horseshoe Cove is not a place you want to fish when the wind is blowing hard from the west or northwest. These directions will put the wind right in your face and make it difficult to get the distance you need from your casts. Wind can also make the fishing uncomfortable in the early part of the season, because the colder water temperatures quickly chill the air.

Horseshoe Cove—along with Spermaceti Cove, just below it—are two areas that you definitely want to fish by boat. Captain Dave Chouinard, owner of the Fly Hatch in Shrewsbury, was born and bred along these waters and is considered by many one of the top-producing captains in the area. He teams up with Captain Dick Dennis to give clients a productive alternative to fishing the ocean when conditions are unfavorable.

This entire area is known for nice catches of stripers, bluefish, and some rather large tide-running weakfish. The most productive times are from the second week in May through the first week in June, and then again from the end of September through the first week of November.

Captain Dave recommends zeroing in first on the waters in and around Skeleton Hill Island. This islands sits in Spermaceti Cove and will produce fish along its edges, drop-offs, cuts, and seams. Use caution as you navigate these waters, however, because hard mussel beds and pilings are pronounced throughout the area. Captain Dave also mentions that if you try to chase fish pushing onto the flats, you can quickly run aground. In shallower areas he recommends a kayak.

A second location to check out is the end of the pilings along the beach as you move north. Here Captain Dave mentions that you'll find an unusual hole with sheer edges that drops quickly from 8 to 20 feet. Once again, work the edges and drop-offs of this hole.

As you move north into Horseshoe Cove, Captain Dave recommends fishing the waters directly adjacent to the artillery bunker. At high tide you'll find water depths in the 8- to 10-foot range as well as a lot of underwater structure and pilings. The remains of an old pier extend outward from this point for a couple of hundred yards. There's excellent fluke fishing here in summer, but it can get very crowded on weekends, when many sailboats take up moorings.

Captain Dave adds a special note to exercise extreme caution in this part of the bay when a wind-against-tide situation sets up—that is, a strong northwest wind blowing against a high outgoing tide. It's not uncommon to see standing wave swells in the 4- to 5-foot range. Such swells can quickly capsize or endanger any small boat.

To get to Horseshoe Cove, travel 3.5 miles down the main roadway once you enter Sandy Hook. At this point you'll see the Horseshoe Cove parking area on your right. Park and walk across the street to the footbridge.

Working the boat channels around any of New Jersey's backwater bridges is extremely productive. Captain Dick Dennis, of the Fly Hatch, shows how it's done. Jim Freda photo.

SANDY HOOK BAY

ROMER SHOAL/FLYNNS KNOLL/RARITAN REACH

The waters adjacent to the tip of Sandy Hook comprise what's known as Sandy Hook Bay. This bay system is only a small part of the much larger Raritan Bay system that's also part of the New York Bight. The New York Bight, in turn, includes New York Harbor's Lower Bay, Jamaica Bay, Sandy Hook Bay, and the Atlantic Ocean coastal waters out to the continental shelf.

Three locations in this area are commonly targeted by boaters, and they constitute some of the finest fishing grounds along our coast. These are Romer Shoal, Flynns Knoll, and the Raritan Reach.

If you head due east 1.8 miles from the tip of Sandy Hook you'll run directly into the Romer Shoal Lighthouse. Hauntingly perched in the middle of what seems like nowhere, this historic lighthouse has stood off the shore of Staten Island since 1898. It stands 54 feet tall and is situated in the middle of a small rock jetty. During World War I the navy stationed personnel in the lighthouse to keep track of vessels entering and leaving the harbor.

The waters directly around the lighthouse jetty are deep, averaging from 16 to 18 feet. Just to the south, however, the water shoals up to around 6 feet. This is an excellent location for fluke, because boaters can anchor up or drift over these shallower waters.

Still, the striped bass is the main quarry targeted around the lighthouse. The best time to fish this area is from June through September; it's not known for early-season action. The majority of the fish are in the 18- to 26-inch range, but much larger fish are frequently caught. The preferred method is bunker chunking or drifting sandworms. (Trolling is unusual here.) White bucktails tipped with pork rinds are also very effective, as is fly fishing— these stripers are more than willing to hit a fly.

I had the pleasure of fishing this area with my friend Captain Dino Torino of Fin Chaser Charters. Along with his partner Captain Frank Crescetelli, Dino does everything first class, right down to their pickup service for clients along the Manhattan and Jersey City waterways. Captain Dino quickly showed me how the long rod could outfish the bunker chunkers two to one. His secret is to use 27 to 30 feet of Cortland's lead-core line as a fast-sinking head. To this he attaches a short leader of 15-pound test to get his flies down quickly. The flies he recommends are marabou minnows or flat-winged Clouser Minnows.

Captain Dino's boating skills were exceptional as he nosed his boat right up to the rocks along the edge of the lighthouse and let the current drift the boat back. This would allow our lines to sink deep close to the drop-offs. As we retrieved back to the boat, the bass would hit just as the fly was moving up and through the rip line around the light. Captain Dino stresses the need for moving water when fishing in this area.

He adds that this spot is not known for holding weakfish, but blues frequently visit. False albacore are also present in fall, particularly when the spearing congregate in these currents. The best time to fish Romer Shoal is during the week; the weekends, especially in summer, are very crowded.

Directly across to the south of Romer Shoal is a rather large area of water known as Flynns Knoll. It's a mile or so in diameter and is adjacent to Sandy Hook Channel. Water depths range from 20 to 27 feet, with deeper surrounding water. Flynns Knoll is one of the most popular places for boaters to anchor up and fish for bass or blues. Most of the bottom in this area is covered with mussels, clams, and worms—a rather attractive habitat for stripers to stick their noses.

The quality and quantity of fish on the knoll change with the seasons. In spring and fall the largest bass will be present. Teen- to 40-pound fish can be caught at these times. In summer there's a good population of fish in the 26- to 32-inch range; larger fish are less common. You'll also see good bluefish and fluke catches throughout the season.

The preferred method for fishing Flynns Knoll is to anchor up and to fish bunker chunks in a chum slick. A very effective method is to position three or four boats side by side to create a large chum slick. Once the bass or blues get tuned into a slick, the bite can be fast and furious. Nonstop action with multiple hook-ups is common.

CHUMMING

When you're chumming, it's important to keep your slick going—but pay attention to the amount of chum you're throwing. You don't want to feed the fish; you want them to search out your baits. Overchunking will produce fewer takes, while underchunking will put the fish in someone else's slick.

You can use just about anything for chunks—bunker, mackerel, herring, and bluefish parts all work. You should also use a chum pot in combination with tossing small chunks over the side of the boat. A good trick is to lower your chum pot to the level of your baits—most likely the bottom. Keeping the pot just over the side of the boat will cause most of the chum to drift over the top of your fishing range.

If you see a good number of boats with slicks set up, position your boat downcurrent and reap some of the benefits. Make sure, however, that you maintain a good distance from these boats: It's not proper etiquette to be in someone else's slick. You shouldn't even drive through one when moving around.

Pay attention to the size of the chunks on your hook also. If the fish are on the small side, your chunks should be sized appropriately. The larger bass will hit both small and large chunks. It's not uncommon to be close to boats that are hooking up when you aren't; in fact, it can be rather frustrating at times. If this happens, check your bait to make sure it hasn't washed out. The fresher the chunk, the better. Fish can hold in a slick for quite some time, but some will eventually find yours.

The bite usually begins on the knoll once the tide starts to move. Moving water is important. If you anchor your boat up during a slack or slow-moving tide, make sure you give yourself enough scope. Otherwise, when the tide begins to rip, your anchor will slip and you'll drift away.

During a moving tide you'll need a 2- to 3-ounce bank sinker to get your baits to the bottom. At other times less weight can be used. When the tide is approaching slack, remove all the weight and let your chunks free drift down into the water column. A 4/0 to 7/0 bait hook is preferred with a 20- to 25-pound-test leader. If some really big cows are around you may want to beef your leader up to 30 or 40 pounds. In fall many boaters also fish at night with live eels for these lunker linesiders. Like Romer Shoal, Flynns Knoll can get very crowded, particularly on weekends. You'll have no problem spotting the fleet.

To the west of Flynns Knoll is the Raritan Reach East channel. This channel runs from New Jersey across to Staten Island, where it becomes the Raritan Reach West channel. It's well known as a favorite weakfish spot from May to August, and will also produce large bass in spring and fall and fluke throughout the summer. The channel averages 27 to 40 feet deep.

Trolling with bunker spoons and wire line is the preferred method for big bass in spring and fall. Jigging bucktails with pork rind is also very effective. It's not uncommon to see fish in excess of 40 pounds come by either of these methods. For weakfish jigging Fin-S Fish in pink or yellow has been a favorite producer, as is drifting sandworms. Your traditional squid and killie combo, along with sand eels, fluke chunks, or sea robin belly, is always good for a doormat fluke. Four- to 7-pound fish are frequently taken.

When working in and around Sandy Hook Bay, you'll need to know whether you're in New Jersey or New York waters. Your location will dictate which marine fishery laws you'll have to adhere to. Drifting over the invisible boundary line from New Jersey to New York can severely impact your wallet if you're found in violation of any of New York's stricter regulations.

As quoted by John Geiser in the *Asbury Park Press*, the "dividing line begins at the Boundary Light, 1.6 miles at 78 degrees magnetic from the mouth of Morgan Creek, and runs straight to Romer Shoal Light, or 2.3 miles at 18 degrees magnetic from the Sandy Hook Channel Buoy just west of the point."

The best advice I can give is to keep aware of your location; most of the marine law enforcement personnel have zero tolerance for any violations.

The Romer Shoal Lighthouse, perched in the middle of Sandy Hook Bay, is one of the landmarks separating New Jersey and New York waters. Jim Freda photo.

TWIN RIVERS

NAVESINK RIVER/SHREWSBURY RIVER/OCEANIC BRIDGE

The tremendous numbers of fishing opportunities in the Sandy Hook area often overshadow the excellent fishery in two of its feeder rivers. The Navesink and Shrewsbury Rivers, also known as the Twin Rivers, are located in the southeastern corner of Sandy Hook Bay. The lower end of these two rivers converges within 1/2 mile of the coast just on the west side of Ocean Avenue in the town of Sea Bright. Both rivers are well known for the early-spring and late-fall fishery that brings trophy stripers, weakfish, blues, and fluke to the scales.

Both rivers are best fished with a small boat, because the access points on foot are limited. Those places that are accessible are well-guarded secrets by many of the locals, although with a bit of investigative work you can find spots that are wadable and extremely productive.

The banks of the Navesink in its lower end are rolling tree-topped hills laden with the sprawling, luxurious homes of the rich and famous. Breathtaking views and lollipop-colored foliage, particularly in fall, make the Navesink one of the most picturesque coastal rivers in the state. A picture of you with a trophy linesider or weakie with Mother Nature's exquisite backdrop will be without question one of the favorites in your scrapbook. Definitely bring your camera when you fish this location.

I spent many a day on these beautiful waters with one of the local experts, my good friend Augie Scafidi. Augie showed me the ins and outs of these locations. The lower section of the Navesink is a key place to be in early spring. Starting in early April and extending right through June you'll find excellent striper, weakfish, and bluefish action. I'm not just talking about small schoolie fish; I'm referring to teen- to 30-pound bass, 4- to 15-pound weakfish, and jumbo blues that will tip the scales in the 8- to 10-pound range. As with any of our coastal rivers across the state, the waters warm quickly in spring due to their shallow depths and muddy bottoms. As a result, the bait will migrate here en masse. The predominant forage for trophy predators is moss-bunker, herring, silversides (spearing), and grass shrimp.

Bunker start pouring into Raritan Bay as early as the end of March and quickly disperse in every direction, moving up and around the tip of the hook to both the Navesink and Shrewsbury Rivers. These bunker are easily noticeable, particularly in the early-morning hours and late at night. Large pods of these baits will be seen and heard on the surface as they make their characteristic flipping commotion. If the pods are tightly schooled, it's a clear indication that the predators are below selectively picking off any individuals that appear injured or disoriented. If the pods are spread out, however, the baits are more relaxed and not being harassed. When bass and blues are on the bunker you'll witness some incredible eruptions as they bust through the baits.

Snagging a bunker with a weighted treble hook or bunker snag and live-lining it is the preferred method for hooking into the largest fish in the area. It's best to have two rods ready for this operation, one set up for snagging and one ready to transfer the bait to for live-lining. Hook the bait on a size 5/0 to 7/0 short-shank hook placed just in front of the dorsal. Don't penetrate below the dorsal too deeply or you'll hit the spine and kill the bait. Allow the bait to swim freely away on a light drag, or by using thumb control with a conventional reel. There will be no doubt when a take occurs: The bunker will begin to flee in a desperate attempt to escape. Line will scream from your reel as the bait is inhaled. Give a 5- to 10-count before you set the hook, and then lean back with considerable force on the rod. Don't be afraid to drive the hook home.

Another remarkable predator–prey relationship occurs in early spring when bass and weaks are on the grass shrimp. During the flood stages of high tide thousands of shrimp will be dislodged from their grass beds, triggering a feeding response. At night when the wind is down and the boats are gone you can walk along the bank and hear the sipping and slurping of bass and weaks dining on these tasty morsels. If you shine a flashlight in the water, you'll be able to see these shrimp scurrying around.

Here is where the fly fisher is at a distinct advantage, because he can throw patterns to "match the hatch." Small rust or brown Clousers tied on 1/0 hooks with black dumbbell eyes work well. The Popovics Ultra Shrimp is another pattern you don't want to be without.

If you're wading you'll need to explore the access points, because much of the river is bordered by private property. One spot definitely worth a mention, however, is just on the upriver side of the Oceanic Bridge. You'll need to cross the bridge to the Middletown side and park along the roadway on the right. There's limited parking; the area will accommodate only about six cars. From this point you need to walk along the beach back to the bridge's main overpass. Walk under the overpass; you'll be on a flat about 2 feet deep. You can walk this flat straight out to the channel. Here the water drops off quickly to 12 feet.

You can cast from the flat into the channel. Drifting Fin-S Fish or bucktail jigs in this current is very effective. You can also fish flies on quick-sinking lines. When the blues are around, white Twister Tails will quickly put you into fish, because they stand out in the sometimes stained river water. Plugs and small metal will also score one blue after another.

A small boat is by far the best way to cover the waters along the Twin Rivers. From the Oceanic Bridge in the Navesink to the Highlands Bridge in the Shrewsbury you'll have just over 3 miles of very productive water. At the channel split buoy where the two rivers converge just above the Highlands Bridge, the average channel depth is 20 feet. This area is known as Rocky Point. Opposite the point is a submerged jetty that separates the two river channels. It's clearly marked with four white cans with black diamonds.

One of the first locations to check in the Navesink is what locals call the weakfish hole. It's found just upriver of the Oceanic Bridge on the north side of the river and is marked by Buoy 17. The hole drops off to 20 feet deep. Use your fishfinder to locate the hole and you'll no doubt see fish sitting there for the taking. Use the current and wind to drift through the hole.

Farther upriver, just outside Red Bank, is another favorite weak-fish hole at Buoy 20.

Directly under the Oceanic Bridge you'll find a 15-foot depth and good quick drop-offs close to the bridge abutments. These abutments are favorite locations for bass to hold while lying in wait to ambush any prey that drifts by. Try casting a bucktail jig between the abutments to pick off some of these bass.

Just below the bridge by Buoy 15A is the bluefish hole, as locals know it. It's on the north side of the channel and drops off to about 10 feet. Here you'll find bluefish corralling and pinning bait against the side of the bar that surrounds the hole. These blues can turn a boring day into a lot of fun. As you head downriver past the 15A hole on your way to the bay, make sure you stay in the channel, which winds and turns as it weaves its way through sandbars on both sides. Trying to take a shortcut will only result in running aground.

A final spot to try is just under the Highlands Bridge—a great location to hook into a trophy bass. The swift currents that move through here mean you'll need to anchor by tying off on one of the wooden bridge pilings. Be sure you don't anchor in the channel, and be careful to avoid the underground cable in the area, which you can get caught up on. Bunker chunking or eeling is the way to fish here. You'll need to use enough weight to get down in the current. The depth directly under the bridge is 25 feet.

In the Shrewsbury River work the waters from the Highlands Bridge upriver to the Sea Bright Bridge. My friend Captain Bill Hoblitzell of Outback Fishing Charters has been guiding on these waters for years and highly recommends this stretch. Captain Bill says that drifting live baits such as worms, herring, bunker, eels, spots, or snappers is the preferred method, but cut baits and chunks are also very effective.

Captain Bill also points out that blind casting flies, plugs, bucktails, or soft baits into the light shadows of the numerous docks and bulkheads that line this 2.5-mile stretch of river will put a lot of fish in your boat. He recommends fishing at night, when the boat traffic is at a minimum.

Downriver at Rocky Point Captain Bill advises fishing the edge of the rips that form along the submerged jetty on either side of the changing tides. He cautions not to run between the cans that mark the jetty, however, because you can damage your lower boat unit.

To get to the mouth of the Shrewsbury and Navesink Rivers, follow Ocean Avenue through Sea Bright and head toward Sandy Hook. The Shrewsbury River is on your left. There are private marinas where you can launch a boat for a fee.

To get to the Oceanic Bridge wading flats, take West River Road through Rumson until you get to Bingham Road and make a left. Go over the bridge; as you approach the Middletown side, you'll see a small parking area on the right-hand side.

SHREWSBURY ROCKS
MONMOUTH BEACH/GAS CAN

A wide variety of bottom topography makes up the inshore waters along the Jersey coast—from sandy lumps to shoals, ridges, and extensive clam or mussel beds. You'll come across areas that are relatively flat and featureless, while others are rock covered with diverse forms of marine life inhabiting every tiny nook and cranny. One inshore area of particular interest to the New Jersey angler is the Shrewsbury Rocks, located off Monmouth Beach in northern Monmouth County. The Shrewsbury Rocks are well known among the striper elite as one of the prime locations in all of New Jersey for producing trophy bass. They're also a unique piece of structure; there's nothing else like them along the entire New Jersey coast.

The Shrewsbury Rocks are found in a wide area of rocky bottom that stretches from 14 down to 50 feet deep. The hard, irregular bottom can be easily identified on your fishfinder as you approach the rocks. If you use loran numbers, 635.0 puts you at the southern side of the rocks, which extend out to 947.0. There are also two buoys in place to notify shipping vessels of the shallow water. The inshore buoy is approximately 1 mile out and is known as the Can. The outer buoy is about 2 miles out; it's called the Gas Can.

Trophy stripers and jumbo blues are the targets of the boaters jigging, chunking, eeling, or trolling these rocks. All of these methods will produce fish throughout the season. Many anglers also opt to anchor up on the rocks and start a chum slick with bunker parts and chunks, while others sneak out under the cover of darkness on a cool autumn evening and drift eels over the bottom. And still others opt for the heavy hardware, trolling big bunker spoons or umbrella rigs to bring their quarry up from the depths.

One individual well known throughout New Jersey as a striper expert is Joe Nunziato. Joe describes himself as "a man mystically possessed with a dedicated reverence for striped bass fishing." He has plugged almost all of our New Jersey rock piles, soaked clams up and down the coast, and trolled an endless number of miles in search of that trophy bass. To his credit he has landed 20 striped bass of more than 40 pounds; the largest was 48 pounds, 6 ounces.

I am fortunate enough to be friends with Joe and he graciously gave me the tour of the Rocks while revealing some of his best-guarded secrets for wire line trolling. These tips and techniques have taken Joe thousands of hours of trolling to perfect.

To begin with, you need the right equipment: a metal-spooled reel loaded with 100 to 300 feet of 50- to 80-pound Dacron or mono backing. Add to this 300 feet of 40- to 50-pound Monel or stainless wire. Joe prefers Monel, which is limper and easier to work with despite being slightly more expensive. Your wire should be marked in intervals of 100, 150, 200, and 250 feet so you can judge its depth when it's out behind your boat. A simple formula to remember is that when you're trolling a spoon, the wire will sink at a rate of 1 foot for every 10 feet of wire in the water. Umbrella rigs will go deeper, depending on the number of arms and what you're trolling.

In the end of the wire tie an Albright twist, then add a 20-foot piece of 60- to 80-pound Jinkai or fluorocarbon leader looped into the Albright loop. Knot a heavy-duty ball-bearing snap swivel to the other end of the leader. Use a longer (9 to 10 feet) heavy-action conventional rod for trolling spoons, and a shorter 6- to 8-foot rod for dragging umbrella rigs. Make sure these rods have carborundum guides to stand up to the harsh wire.

Joe's favorite lures when wire-lining for trophy bass are bunker spoons—either big Reliable or Graves. Having the spoon at the same depth that the bass are feeding or cruising is only half the battle. The other consideration is to have the right action on the spoon to elicit strikes. Your spoons should track side to side and not spin. A bass will show little interest in a spinning spoon.

The right action on your spoon will be dictated by your trolling speed. When the desired speed is reached, your rods will be pumping at least 100 times every minute. To get this action, your trolling speed will vary anywhere from 2.5 to 4-plus miles per hour. Take note of the direction that you're trolling when this desired effect is achieved. Changing direction may have you trolling against the current, tide, or wind; you'll have to modify your trolling speed to achieve the right action again.

Another effective technique that Joe has discovered over the years is trolling a pair of identical spoons. If you're using a Graves spoon on one rod, use a Graves spoon on the other rod, too. Different brands of spoons require different trolling speeds, and move differently. Having two spoons that are alike will minimize tangles and headaches. Joe also points out that most spoons track approximately 6 feet from side to side, so you need to place your rods in a pair of outrodders to give the spoons enough space. This will also eliminate tangles. Joe likes big colorful spoons that throw as much flash as possible, along with added noise and vibration. When trolling deep in relatively clear water, the orb of light around the spoon will be approximately 10 feet in all directions.

Joe highly recommends attaching safety leashes to your rods when trolling bunker spoons. In fall a large bass can strike out viciously at your spoons and easily pull with enough force to rip your rod into the water. With the safety attached, you can recover the rod by pulling it in.

When trolling umbrella rigs Joe uses either shad bodies or tubes. In either case he places a 10- to 12-foot leader behind the umbrella with a large plug attached. This trailing plug is usually what a really big bass will hit, because the umbrella gets its attention. Joe likes to use shad bodies in the 5- to 6-inch range. For single tubes he likes dark red 12 inches or larger. Many times he tips the tubes with sandworms to increase strikes. With tubes it's important to get your trolling speed down to 2 miles per hour or less.

Large wooden plugs can also be effectively trolled on a wire outfit. Here Joe uses a shorter rod and a 10- to 15-foot leader on the wire. A snap—not a snap swivel—is used to connect the plug to the leader.

When you're fighting a bass on a wire outfit, Joe points out that it's extremely important not to pump the rod. Each time the rod is pumped, slack is created in the line that opens the hook hole in the fish's mouth. This makes it easier for the hook to fall out.

Joe also advocates having a good sense of etiquette, direction, and spatial awareness when trolling at the rocks. Nothing is more annoying than to have an inexperienced boater come too close and cross over your lines. Keep at least 100 yards from other boats. If you're going to cross behind another boat, radio the captain and ask for permission. Also, slow down when approaching the rocks and other boats. If a captain is set up and trolling and has to stop or slow down, his rigs are going to fall to the bottom and get hopelessly snagged in the rocks. Use good common sense; it's a big ocean with plenty of room for everyone.

To get to the Shrewsbury Rocks, travel 16 miles north out of the Manasquan Inlet, 10 miles north out of the Shark River Inlet, or 7 to 10 miles south from Sandy Hook.

DEAL LAKE FLUME
EIGHTH AVENUE JETTY/
JETTY COUNTRY/T-JETTY, ALLENHURS T

In the northern part of Monmouth County you'll find Deal Lake nestled between the towns of Deal and Asbury Park. The lake has an outflow to the ocean located right at the Eighth Avenue Jetty in Asbury Park. This outflow, or flume as the locals know it, serves as one of the first locations in Monmouth County that hosts big stripers each April and May.

This excellent early-season striper run is attributed to and coincides with the historical arrival of *Alosa pseudoharengus* and *A. aestivalis*, better known as the alewife and blueback herring, respectively. Since the alewife and blueback are anadromous in nature, their primordial instincts drive them to return to fresh water to spawn. In early spring this natural occurrence goes on through-out our state wherever a freshwater river, lake, creek, or pond is open to the ocean by way of inlets or man-made structures.

Alewifes and bluebacks are the filet mignon of a striper's diet when compared to the diverse range of baitfish and morsels these predators consume. The baits can be easily captured at their freshwater spawning grounds with dip nets, herring darts, or small gold hooks. Areas like the Deal flume are ideally suited for catching these baits because of the extremely narrow entrance point that the baits must pass through to enter the lake.

Look for the herring to stage and school up on the ocean side of the flume and then make a mass migration during the full- and new-moon phases of the early-spring months. The increased water level and tidal flow during these periods helps stimulate the run. You should check the current regulations in the *NJ Freshwater Compendium* in regard to the number of herring that can legally be taken, and on which dates. Regulations can change from year to year.

Using live herring as bait is one of the most productive ways to lure a trophy springtime bass. The Eighth Avenue Jetty directly in front of the flume is an ideal location for live-lining. When fishing this area you're bound to run into some members of the Asbury Park Fishing Club, because this is their home turf. This club is comprised of some of the most experienced anglers in all of New Jersey. Established in 1889, it's the oldest fishing club in the country, and today has approximately 100 members.

A familiar face along these rocks is the club's president for the past 16 years, Joe Pallotto. Joe has been pounding the surf for more than 40 years and has scored some very large bass in his day. His largest to date is a 48 1/2-pounder caught from the surf on a live herring. Joe recalls the days when the action around the Deal flume was nothing short of phenomenal: 30- and 40-pound bass were common in early spring. These big bass would always show up on the tail end of the spring mackerel run.

Today, Joe says, the action is different. Now we're seeing fish mostly in the 10- to 12-pound range, with the bigger fish going up to 25 pounds. He adds that picking a spot in front of the flume is the key to your success. Joe tactfully refers to this area as the "restaurant"—a reference to the traffic of bait moving in and out.

The fishery remains consistent until the middle of June, but angling usually starts around the end of March; these baits start to show in the area around St. Patrick's Day. Joe's setup is a 9 1/2-foot Lamiglas rod with a conventional 7700 Ambassadeur reel. He uses 20-pound mono tied directly to a 5/0 Gamakatsu hook.

Knowing when to set the hook is one of the most important keys to your success. Over the years Joe's learned to tell by feel when it's the correct time to drive the steel home. For beginners he recommends giving a slow count to 10, then locking down the reel. Take in the slack until the line draws tight, then set the hook.

The arrival of big bass also stirs the attention of the saltwater fly rodder. The close proximity of the numerous jetties north and south of the flume entrance puts the fly rodder away from the crowds and advantageously within striking distance.

Given the bigger and bulkier flies you'll need to imitate the wider profile of the herring, use a 10- or 11-weight rod.

A trick to help entice strikes with your fly is to tie it to the leader with a loop knot. This will ensure that the fly undulates from side to side as it's held in the current alongside the jetty. Big bass are notorious for ambushing these baits right along the rocks.

Effective flies for the alewife should be tied in greenish hues with a bronze back. For the blueback, as the name implies, add a bluish hue or tint to its dorsal surface. Keep in mind, however, that these baitfish reflect light from many different portions of the visible spectrum, which is dispersed throughout the water column. When you see the bait out of the water, it looks different to some degree from what the bass see under the water. For this reason some savvy long rodders incorporate many hues into their fly designs. Purple, lavender, or even pink will add a nice touch to the basic foundation colors. Tie in a bit of flash and you've got just what you need to get that trophy to strike out at your fly rather than the real thing.

This entire stretch of beach—through Deal and the surrounding towns of Long Branch to the north and Asbury Park to the south—has been known for years as Jetty Country. The close proximity and the length of the groins (their technical name) have attracted many a jetty jock over the years. In one outing it's quite easy to "jetty-hop" from one rock pile to the next, thoroughly plugging half a dozen or so in a four-hour period. Recent beach replenishment projects have changed the topography of these treasured grounds to a great degree, however.

Just to the north of the flume in the little town of Allenhurst you'll find the T-Jetty, well known for its shape. This jetty juts out into the ocean, where its T section parallels the beach for a good distance. When the wind is out of the west and the water is calm, this T extension is an ideal location to stand and cast or to fly fish with the wind at your back. A nice pocket is also present where schools of bait get pinned, making themselves easy prey for bass and weakfish.

A word of caution is in order when hitting any of the rock piles along this stretch of beach. Many of these groins are not flat topped like the longer jetties around our inlets. Rather, they're jagged and irregular in shape. Walking out on these rocks can be outright dangerous. Experienced jetty jocks wear Korkers, which are carbide-steel-studded sandals that fit over your boots. Korkers will give you sure footing when you walk out on the wet, alga-covered rocks. They're an absolute must for safety and will help prevent you from slipping or taking an unfortunate spill. Don't even think about walking out on a jetty without them.

Every year in this area there is a yearlong Interclub Striper Tournament in which eight local clubs jockey for top honors. Besides the Asbury Park Club you'll find the Spring Lake Live Liners, Berkeley Striper Club, Shark River Anglers, Bradley Beach Fishing Club, Steven's Surfsters, Monmouth Beach Cartoppers, and Team Mullet competing. This tournament coincides with the spring and fall striper runs along the beach. At the end of the season a grand champion is crowned.

To get to the Deal Lake flume, travel north on Main Street through Asbury Park until you reach Deal Lake. Make a right and head straight to the end of the road. The flume will be on your left. There's a dirt parking lot with ample space at this point.

To get to the T-Jetty in Allenhurst, continue around Deal Lake to Ocean Avenue. Travel several blocks to Cedar Avenue and make a right. Go straight up to the beach; you'll see the T-Jetty directly in front of you.

Korkers are an absolute must for safety when fishing any of the many jetties that can be found across our state. Shell E. Caris photo.

SHARK RIVER INLET
TIP/L-JETTY/POCKET

Seventeen miles south of Sandy Hook is the first navigable entrance to our back bay waters: the Shark River Inlet. This small inlet is bordered to the north by the town of Avon by the Sea and to the south by Belmar. The inlet is commonly referred to as extending from the Oceanic Bridge east to the ends of the North and South Jetty walls that harbor its entrance.

The North Jetty of the inlet is much easier for the shore-bound angler to fish than the South Jetty. The reason is that when standing on the North Jetty, you're much closer to the surface of the water than you are on the South Jetty. Its lower height and the fact that there are fewer jetty rocks extending out in front of you make fighting and landing a fish much more manageable.

The North Jetty is L shaped. As you walk to its end, the jetty juts out parallel to the ocean just before the beacon light for about 100 feet. The rocks have plenty of poured concrete between them so there are very few holes to hinder your walking. This also makes the North Jetty a very safe platform for casting. You must exercise caution when there's any kind of surf, however, because surging waves will break along these rocks and wash over them. At these times the South Jetty is a better bet because of its relatively safer height above the water's surface.

The North Jetty provides fishing access to both the ocean side and the inlet, whereas on the South Jetty you're limited to fishing the inlet or its mouth. The shoaling of sand along its southern ocean side has filled a very nice pocket that once existed.

Three locations on the North Jetty are considered good points to position yourself for a strategic attack. First is the jetty's tip. From here you'll be able to fan cast along a 180-degree plane to work the ocean waters, the mouth of the inlet, and inside the inlet itself. When the tide is ebbing and flowing to the north, throwing a weighted bucktail jig tipped with a Fin-S Fish into the current and allowing it to drift out and around the tip is highly productive. Bass sit and wait in the current for the inlet's tide to deliver a variety of offerings right to their mouths.

The second spot to attack is the pocket right where the main jetty and the L extension meet. To fish here, position yourself at the base of the pocket on the main jetty and cast parallel to the L extension. Work your plug or jig slowly along these rocks, covering the water right to the very edge. There are several flat rocks close to the water along this section that you can walk down to and easily land a fish.

The third spot to set up at is at the tip of the L extension. From here you can cast to the inside toward the beach or straight out into the ocean. A nice pocket has developed behind this point that's always worth investigating.

All the species mentioned in the text can be caught from either jetty of the Shark River Inlet, but there's one time of year when this location produces consistently good numbers of stripers: the end of the season, when most anglers have already put their gear away or turned their attention to the Christmas holidays. From the last two weeks of December into the first two weeks of January you'll find stripers prowling the waters around the North Jetty. Fish will be present until the stiff northwest winds usher in the arctic blasts that drive the water temperature down below 45 degrees.

At this time of year the fishery is not a daytime event. Focus your attention on the nighttime hours during the incoming tide. If the tide crests around midnight, the hours from 8 P.M. on will be good. Since the North Jetty is very safe to walk on, going out on it at night with a flashlight is no problem. The typical northwest winds at this time of year will keep the surf flat, and crashing waves are rare. Go with a partner to be safe, however, since you'll very rarely see anyone else out.

The end of the season is the time to throw large blue- or black-backed Bombers with clear bellies. Yozuris crystal minnows and Megabait plugs are also good choices. These artificials nicely imitate the sea herring that are present at this time. Fishing a large teaser 3 to 4 feet above your plug usually results in doubleheaders.

As you move into the inlet, you'll find three bridges that are worth investigating: from east to west, the Ocean Avenue Bridge, the Main Street Bridge, and the Route 35 Bridge. The Ocean Avenue and Main Street Bridges can be fished on foot. There are some access points underneath these bridges, but they're limited. The Route 35 Bridge is better left to the local sharpies.

Fishing under and around these structures can be highly productive for some big bass. Bridge fishing is a completely different art than fishing from the surf or jetty. The massive amounts of rubble and snags underneath these structures require special tackle and tactics. Most anglers use heavy-duty spin or conventional rods loaded with 80-pound braid. Strong leaders in the 50- to 60-pound class are also necessary, because a hooked bass will head for any obstruction in an effort to break off. You'll need to keep a bass from getting down into these obstructions if you're to have any chance to land it.

Fishing under the bridges by boat is also a very effective way to hook into some quality-sized bass. This type of fishing is going to be limited to times when the channel isn't busy—usually in the very early morning, or at night.

These three bridges are especially productive in fall, from the middle to the end of October, when large bass hole up underneath. Chunking is the most effective way to catch them.

You need to position your boat just at the top of the deep holes under the bridges. Anchoring in the channel is illegal, so be careful about how and when you do this. You'll drift your bait back into these holes, so the tide will determine which side of the hole, east or west, you set up on. The best bait is fresh bunker, fished on the bottom during either side of the slack high tide. Once the tide starts running, it will be very difficult to keep your bait in the right place. The bass wiill also relocate during a fast-running tide.

During this slack period your bunker should be filleted; cut 6-inch triangular wedges from its back. Hook these on a strong-shank 7/0 or 8/0 hook by placing the hook in the front of the wedge. Use enough weight to get the bunker wedge to the bottom and allow it to flutter back and forth in the current. It's important that your bait not spin in a circle. Instead it should be undulating from side to side in a slow rhythmic motion.

To get the bass interested in your bait, chum slightly with the remaining pieces of the bunker. Don't overchum: You want the bass to come to your bait and not just sit there as chunks drift slowly back to them for an easy meal. When a bass hits, allow it a moment to take the bait and then set the hook hard, very hard. This is no place to try to play a fish. Instead, rear back on the rod in an effort to keep the bass from heading into the rubble and obstructions that it's seeking.

Use your fishfinder to check the holes under the bridges for holding fish. When the big bass are there, your fishfinder will very clearly show large markings right above the bottom. Now you know you're in business. If you don't see anything on your fishfinder, move along to the next bridge and take a look.

Whether you choose to fish the Shark River Inlet on foot or by boat, the strong tidal flows associated with it are going to dictate your success. Fishing the time period on either side of the slack high or low tide is the best way to get your offerings down deep to work the water column completely.

To get to the Shark River Inlet, head east from any of the major roads that run through Belmar or Avon. Drive along Ocean Avenue to the boundary between the two towns, and you're there. Parking is available right along Ocean Avenue, but it's limited.

SHARK RIVER
MAIN CHANNEL/TENNIS COURTS/NORTH CHANNEL

Many river systems enter the ocean up and down the New Jersey coast. As these rivers flow seaward, their fresh water mixes with the tidal salt water, creating estuary systems at their mouths. These estuary systems serve as the primary nursery grounds for many of the marine fish and invertebrate organisms that inhabit our coast.

These waters are ideally suited for harboring juveniles, because they're sheltered from the wind and rough surf found along our beaches. They also have a limited number of predators when compared to life in the open ocean. These estuaries possess an abundant supply of nutrients, which run off from the surrounding land. This in turn acts as the stimulus for a first trophic level of phytoplankton and zooplankton. These microscopic organisms are responsible for supporting the higher trophic levels and thus establishing a complex food web within the estuary.

All of these nutrient-rich systems will hold resident populations of striped bass, weakfish, and fluke from spring through fall. You'll also find good populations of bluefish, though this species is much more transient. Blues may be present one day and gone the next. Winter flounder also take up residence during the winter and early-spring months.

In early spring ocean fishing is usually on the slow side due to the cold water temperatures. A similar situation can occur in the middle of summer—we've all experienced summer doldrums in the surf. During both these times, however, our river systems remain highly productive, with consistent catches. These are the places to check out.

The Shark River is one of the smaller river systems in New Jersey, but that doesn't make it any less productive. Located in southern Monmouth County, the river empties into the ocean at the Shark River Inlet. On any given summer night you can drift through the river's channels or walk along its banks and watch weakfish and bass bust through schools of spearing. Like many of our rivers, the Shark gets choked with bait by the time August rolls around. Spearing, mullet, peanut bunker, baby snappers and weakfish, bay anchovies, sand eels, shrimp, and crabs are just some of the many baits that can be found. All will school up in the river until they make their mass exodus when the water temperature starts to drop in fall.

Because the Shark River is so shallow, its waters warm quickly in early spring. This in turn triggers feeding by the winter flounder that moved in during the previous early-winter months. At this time these fish are finishing their spawn and refueling for their journey back to the continental shelf. Thus, the Shark River has become well known as an early-season winter flounder hot spot. Some of these winter flatties will tip the scales at 3 pounds, but the majority are in the 1- to 2-pound range.

Winter flounder differ in appearance from their summer cousin the fluke in that they're a right-sided fish and smaller in size. The "top" of the fish is actually its right side. They feed on soft-bodied benthic baits like worms and dislodged mussels, clams, and snails. They have small mouths with no visible teeth. The fluke, on the other hand, is a left-sided fish and can grow quite large. It has a large mouth filled with teeth for attacking small baitfish such as spearing, killies, and sand eels. Larger fluke will also go after baby snappers, weakfish, peanut bunker, mullet—just about anything that swims.

Once the water temperature hits 45 degrees, winter flounder start to move out of the mud in search of food. The key to successful catches during the early part of the season is to anchor up and chum heavily. Boaters who go out with just 1 or 2 chum logs may pick up several fish, but the boater using 8 to 10 chum logs usually catches good numbers. These fish need to be stimulated to feed, and the scent of your chum slick will draw them into your baits. Double anchoring is also very effective: It will prevent your boat from swinging in the current, enabling you to set up a much better chum line.

Chum is usually a mixture of ground-up mussels, clams, snails, corn, and rice that's placed in a chum pot. It can be fresh or frozen. The pot is lowered over the side of the boat and set on the bottom. It will slowly milk out as the current runs through the wire mesh of the chum pot. You should occasionally bounce the pot off the bottom to turn the chum in the pot so it can continue to milk. Additional chum can be dropped overboard, but take care not to just give the fish a free meal. The key is for them to find your baits.

You can use conventional or spinning gear for winter flounder fishing; it's a matter of personal preference. Whichever tackle you choose, make sure it's on the light side. Surf or jetty rods really have no place when it comes to winter flounder. A 5- to 7-foot light-action rod spooled with no more than 10-pound test is all you need. Many veteran anglers will opt for 6- or 8-pound test. For hooks you can use the traditional long-shank Chestertown or the now popular Mustad or Gamakatsu size 8 or 9 wide-gap hook. These hooks are snelled and tied onto a 3- or 4-foot leader, with one hook tied on with a dropper loop. This is then tied to a three-way swivel. Use a bank sinker or dipsey weight to get the rig to the bottom. You should occasionally bounce the bottom with the weight to stir up the mud. This will help attract flounder to your baits.

Many anglers work two rods at a time by holding one in each hand and alternately lifting and lowering them until they feel a take. Setting the hook requires a little more feel and finesse than does setting the hook on a striper. If you strike hard, you'll undoubtedly pull the hook out of the flounder's mouth. Instead you should slowly direct the rod tip in the direction of the take and then reel down two or three turns and set the hook with a short, quick strike.

There are several locations that are very productive in the early part of the season. First is the channel located adjacent to the tennis courts in Maclearie Park. This channel runs parallel to Route 35 South. This area can be fished by boat or from a newly created fishing walkway that runs along its length.

The main channel runs along the marina and has a very popular bulkhead on its east side. There's plenty of parking in this area along with a boat launch that can be used for a fee. The area in front of the gas docks here contains some of the deeper holes

The Shark River is an early–season hot spot for winter flounder. Joe Bayer lands another one of the tasty flatfish. Jim Freda photo.

in the river. There is also a concrete walkway for fishing that's heavily utilized during the peak of the run.

Another excellent location is the channel on the north side of the river; it runs along South Concourse Drive in Neptune. This narrow channel is definitely worth a look. It holds plenty of fish and isn't fished as much as the main channel.

You can access Shark River from Route 35 South or North. Travel until you reach the Belmar Marina and you're there.

SEA GIRT

WRECK POND/BROWN, BEACON, AND NEW YORK AVENUE JETTIES

In the southern part of Monmouth County lies the 1-square-mile coastal community of Sea Girt. Founded in 1875 by a group of Philadelphia land developers, the town is bordered to the north by Wreck Pond, to the south by Stockton Lake, and to the east by the Atlantic Ocean. These three bodies of water form a "girtle" around the town—thus the name, Sea Girt. In the 1800s countless ships were wrecked in the waters near this well-known seaside resort. Ninety-two vessels met their demise in the 1890s alone.

In response to these tragedies the Sea Girt Lighthouse was built at the entrance to Wreck Pond in 1896, then known as the Sea Girt Inlet, to aid ships heading for New York Harbor to the north. (The Sea Girt Inlet was a major thoroughfare for ships heading in from the ocean, but by 1930 it had filled in so much that it became impassable.) The lighthouse was activated on December 10, 1896, and its beacon could be seen piercing the misty Atlantic for 15 miles. Today the Sea Girt Lighthouse Citizens Committee maintains the Sea Girt Lighthouse as a national historic site.

This historic landmark overlooks one of the most productive and quietly kept locations for big bass in Monmouth County. The lighthouse now seems to keep watch protectively over this location that's fished mostly by locals and seldom frequented by outsiders. When the fall blitzes are occurring and the popular barrier beaches to the south become shoulder-to-shoulder anglers, Sea Girt remains wide open with few crowds but excellent fishing.

The area that has been most productive for both surf and boat anglers is centered on the northern end of the beach, in the vicinity of the Wreck Pond flume. This area begins one jetty to the north of the flume in the neighboring town of Spring Lake. Here you'll find the Brown Avenue Jetty. Directly to the south is the flume, followed by the Beacon Avenue and New York Avenue

Jetties, respectively, in Sea Girt.

This area is most productive at two times of the year. In April and May herring arrive at the entrance to the flume; then from the end of June into the first two weeks of July large adult bunker schools are present just off the beach.

As the herring enter Wreck Pond to spawn you'll see a situation similar to the one farther north at the Deal Lake flume. Herring will tend to concentrate at the entrance to the flume and make a consolidated run into the pond during the new- or full-moon phases toward the end of April. The flume at Wreck Pond is actually a 6-foot-wide outflow pipe that empties into the surf zone on the beach. Unlike Deal, there's no jetty next to the flume.

You can fish from the bulkhead that cradles the outflow pipe, but caution must be exercised. The timbers housing the pipe are only about a foot wide and are spaced about 5 feet apart. You'll have to step from the timbers onto the top of the pipe and back to the timbers to reach the end of the flume. Once you're there, the end of the flume can fish two anglers comfortably. Any more than that is not safe.

This location is ideal for one or two fly rodders. You can deliver an unimpeded backcast here; your line will lie out over the water nicely. The pipe's outflow current is nicely suited for using quick-sinking lines or shooting heads. Allowing your fly to drift naturally in the current as it tails out into the surf zone will always get the attention of a hungry striper or toothy blue.

Another method that will produce strikes is to hold your fly in the current without stripping line, allowing it to undulate back and forth. Tying your fly to your leader with a loop knot will provide the greatest range of motion for the fly. In April and May large herring patterns, white Deceivers, Half-and-Halfs, or Snake Flies are the best producers.

The front and sides of the flume are also a favorite location for anglers to cast net or jig for herring. The flume's height above the water makes it very easy to look down and spot where these baits have concentrated. One throw of a cast net can produce all the herring you'll need for live-lining.

Moving north or south of the flume to the adjacent jetties will also produce great results because of their close proximity to its entrance. Bass that are cruising toward the front of the pipe will intercept these jetties on their way. The Brown Avenue Jetty to the north is accessible at low tide despite the recent sand replenishment project. The Beacon and New York Avenue Jetties are accessible during either tide.

All three of these jetties have large rock outcroppings at their tips where the jetty rocks have been dislodged by strong storms. These outcroppings extend out below the water for 20 or 30 yards. These submerged rock piles create an excellent ambush point for stripers to lie in wait for their prey.

Boaters not familiar with the area should be careful not to get too close to the tips of these jetties. There are several spots where the submerged rocks lie only a foot or two below the surface even though it appears you are safe distance from the jetty tip. Position your boat well off their tips and throw your baits or plugs into the area.

Live-lining herring in spring or adult bunker in late summer is the most productive method to hook into a burly linesider. This method will work well from any of these jetties, in front of the pipe, or from a boat. Boaters, however, have the advantage because they can chase down the bait. This is particularly true when the bunker are present in summer. During this time you can expect fish to range in the 20- to 30-pound class, with a good number of teen-sized fish mixed in as well.

Cruising up to a school of bunker and snagging them with a bunker snag is one way to get your bait. Throwing a cast net is the other. The bunker snag is a large, weighted treble hook or series of smaller trebles tied behind a weight that you rip through the bait. Once the bait is snagged, it can be left to sit in the school. A large bass will quickly find this injured bait and viciously strike out at it. Many boaters, however, opt to have two rods set up—one for snagging and the other for live-lining the bait. Once the bait is snagged, it's transferred to the preferred conventional outfit with a single 6/0 or 7/0 short-shank hook. Using the single hook will ensure a better hook set and result in fewer lost fish. The other advantage to the single hook is that any bass you release will have a better chance of survival. A single hook will do much less damage than a treble snag. Allow your bait to swim freely around the jetty tip and be ready to hold on.

During the summertime most public beaches along the Jersey coast do not allow fishing during bathing hours, typically from 9 A.M. to 5 P.M. At the southern end of Sea Girt, however, you'll find a public beach that has been designated fishing only during the day. This beach is just north of Trenton Boulevard and gives you approximately 400 yards of beachfront fishing access. This is a nice place to bring a lounge chair and soak up some sun while you wet a line.

To get to the Sea Girt flume by boat, head north out of the Manasquan Inlet along the beach for 2 miles. From the Shark River Inlet head south for 3 miles. By roadway take Route 71 to Sea Girt Avenue. Go east on Sea Girt Avenue to First Avenue; follow First to Beacon Boulevard and make a right. Drive up to the beach, and you're there.

MANASQUAN INLET
NORTH JETTY/SOUTH JETTY

Many of the tourists who visit the seaside community of Manasquan will include in their vacation a walk out on the North or South Jetty of the Manasquan Inlet. These granite-walled structures were built as a combined county, state, and federal project at the same time that the inlet was being dredged. Completed in 1931, the jetties provided a perpendicular break-water for safely navigating the waters of the inlet. The rocks for the jetties came from the excavation of the Second Avenue sub-way in Manhattan and were shipped on flatbed railroad cars to Sea Girt and trucked two at a time to the inlet.

In 1981 both jetties were extended with 1,343 gigantic concrete jacks, called dolosses, that were nestled together. These 11-foot high, 16-ton erosion-control structures were designed to provide for better protection from storms and to allow sand to flow more freely along the inlet's mouth. This would prevent the sand from getting trapped along the jetty rocks and subsequent-ly filling in its entrance. As some of the dolosses became dam-aged by the inevitable forces of Mother Nature and actually moved away from their intended locations, they were replaced with improved structures known as corelocs, which are heavier and have three flukes at their base instead of two. This provided much more stability and safekeeping from the forces of Mother Nature. In all 29 corelocs were placed on the North Jetty and 18 on the South, interlocking naturally with the existing dolosses.

Fishermen who visit the town of Manasquan make a point of fishing the inlet's North Jetty. This jetty is preferred over the South Jetty because of the lengthy access it provides to the ocean side. The North Jetty puts the surf caster in a more opportune loca-tion to fish ocean waters that would otherwise be inaccessible except by boat. All fishing from the South Jetty is in the inlet's waters, except for small pockets on its south side and at its tip.

Exercise caution when walking out on the North Jetty, because the granite boulders are not sitting tightly together. The spaces that exist between the jetty rocks present a hazard if you're not watching your step. This particular makeup extends for three-quarters of the jetty's length. From this point forward a flat-topped concrete platform can be found that supports the Coast Guard beacon light. This concrete structure is wide and safe, and it provides an excellent vantage point to watch Mother Nature as she tosses huge breakers along the jetties' edges.

The dolosses that form the final quarter of the North Jetty's tip are very dangerous and difficult to walk on. It is not advisable to venture onto these structures. Yes, on any given day you will see numerous fishermen perched on top of them—it's here at the tip that the most fish, stripers and weakfish particularly, hold and can be caught—but landing these fish is extremely difficult, and most attempts result in fish and entire rigs becoming lost.

I've found three locations on the North Jetty productive throughout the season. The first is right at the beginning of the jetty, where the sand and water meet on the ocean side. This area is known as the pocket. At high tide you'll find bass, weakfish, and fluke cruising through here, looking for bait that has been stunned as waves crash onto the beach. The pocket is best known, however, as an excellent autumn ambush point for bass and blues as they pin thousands of southward-migrating mullet and peanut bunker up against the rocks. This is where a fly rodder casting a Popovics's Siliclone Mullet or Geno's Baby Angel bunker pattern can score heavily.

The second location that you'll definitely want to fish is also on the ocean side. This area is three-quarters of the way out on the rocks where the concrete platform begins. This is also where the dolosses begin to extend the jetty. There are several large, flat rocks at this point; you can climb down fairly close to the water when it's not rough. A deep hole directly in front of this spot is a haven for large weakfish and bass in fall.

The third spot is located on the inlet side where the jetty rocks end and the dolosses begin. A deep eddy lies directly in front, providing a haven where baitfish can get out of the swift tidal currents of the inlet. As a result, they become easy prey for any one of our predators. Weighted Fin-S Fish jigs or Smilin' Bill bucktails are great for this location. Cast them out into the main current of the inlet and let them drift naturally into the eddy. As they start to drop down, they'll often provoke a strike.

As productive as the North Jetty is, its main disadvantage for fishing is its height above the water. It can be very difficult to land a fish, which must be lifted up and over the protruding rocks below. For this reason many anglers have adapted long-handled nets or gaffs in the 10- to 12-foot range to reach their quarry. If you try to climb down the rocks to the water's edge, be constantly aware of the approaching breakers. Many anglers have been knocked down or into the water by rogue waves.

The North Jetty is also known as one of the premier spots along the East Coast for surfers due to the characteristic break that refracts around its tip. For this reason the best time to fish is early in the morning before the water gets too crowded. Most of the time surfers use the rip that runs along the side of the rocks as a quick way to get out beyond the break. Cooperation usually exists, and both groups can equally enjoy the benefits of this location.

To get to the North Jetty travel east on Main Street through Manasquan to the beach. Make a left and head south to the inlet. Park along the rail and walk to up to the gazebo. You'll see the jetty from there.

MANASQUAN INLET
MAIN CHANNEL/WILLIS HOLE/POINT PLEASANT

The Manasquan Inlet is located in the heart of central New Jersey and is home to the Manasquan River and estuarine system. Historically the inlet has naturally sought its own opening to the sea by pushing aside sand in response to major northeastern storms. These "nor'easters," as they're known as by the local coastal residents, have moved the inlet's opening as far north as the neighboring town of Sea Girt. The inlet was officially opened for navigational purposes on July 3, 1931, when Frank Stires, of Manasquan, was the first to steer a 16-foot skiff through its channel. Since that time the inlet has served as a haven for recreational, charter, and commercial fishermen. Today it marks the northernmost part of the Intracoastal Waterway.

The main channel of the inlet has an average depth of about 20 feet and is approximately 200 feet wide. The total distance across the inlet from the Manasquan Jetty to the jetty on the Point Pleasant side is approximately 300 feet. At its western end the main channel empties into Fisherman's Cove to the north and Willis Hole Thoroughfare to the south.

To cast completely across the inlet is a significant accomplishment and was first achieved by Rocky Luciano of the Manasquan Fishing Club on Friday, November 7, 1975, at 3:15 P.M. Rocky cast out with a 3-ounce pyramid sinker and spanned the distance from Manasquan to Point Pleasant. This feat is permanently inscribed in the club's archives.

An effective technique for hooking into any of our main fish species is to drift the main channel in a small boat. Eighteen- to 24-foot boats are ideal for this purpose. The best times are early in the morning or late at night when boat traffic is at a minimum. During the summer and early-fall months both recreational fishermen and pleasure craft use the inlet heavily, so drifting its channel then is not advisable.

Because of the strong tidal currents, drifting will be most productive as the tide approaches slack high or low. This will give you the best opportunity to keep your bait close to the bottom. If fluke or winter flounder are your targets, the bottom is where you need to be. You'll need to select the appropriate amount of weight to bounce the bottom as you drift. Not only will the current affect your drift, but the prevailing wind will also have to be factored into the equation. An ideal situation would be an incoming tide with a west wind blowing out. These two forces will tend to cancel one another out, and the result will be a nice steady, slow drift.

All of the main species of fish move through the inlet during the course of a season. Winter flounder move through the inlet starting in October and continuing into December. They then move into the Manasquan River searching out suitable spawning grounds for winter. In spring bass, weakfish, and fluke arrive and remain until the end of fall. These fish move back and forth from the estuary to the ocean ambushing baits trapped by the strong tidal flows. Large bluefish rarely move through the inlet with any kind of regularity. Because of their pelagic nature, they appear unpredictably. However, a resident population of small 1- to 2-pound fish can usually be found. In late summer and early fall you'll always find an abundant snapper population well established.

Another notable occurrence that takes place from the end of August through the early part of September is the arrival of false albacore, Spanish mackerel, bullet mackerel, and bonito. These fish are fast and will rip line from your reel in a flash. They're very skittish when there's a lot of boat traffic, though. Boaters who eyeball a school of fish and motor up to them will no doubt drive them down. The trick is to dead drift your boat and wait for the fish to come to you. The hot location to position your boat is at the inlet's mouth just outside the jetty rocks on its north side.

Once these fish find the bait they stay with it, feeding in a cyclical fashion. In other words, they'll be right there in front of you and then gone, only to return in a short period of time. If the weather remains consistent and calm for a while, even skipjack tuna will make an appearance.

During the fluke and flounder seasons many small–boaters anchor just off the main channel's west end in the southwest corner. Known as the Willis Hole Thoroughfare, this is the beginning of the charter fishing fleet's channel. A deep hole located at this spot is a prime location for both winter and summer flatties.

As the fluke migrate out of the Manasquan River in late fall, they tend to stage in the inlet's main channel for about a week. The same is true of the winter flounder when they make their move offshore in late spring. Both of these times will present a short window of opportunity, but boaters who are on top of things will find themselves into the biggest flounder of the season.

If you don't have a boat, there's excellent access to the inlet from either the Manasquan or the Point Pleasant side. Both areas offer long rock jetties that take you out to the easternmost end of the inlet. Both sides also have walkways that provide plenty of access to the middle and back portions of the inlet. On the Manasquan side this area is well railed and safe for children to fish from. There's no rail on the Point Pleasant side, but you will find a concrete bulkhead that comes up to about the waistline of a normal adult. Children can fish from behind this, but it's not safe for them to walk along its top.

At the western end of the Point Pleasant side of the inlet you'll come to a small public park named Loughran Point. This area has been dedicated to the memory of Councilman Thomas F. Loughran, who was a strong advocate of the public's right to access the waterfront. Here a wooden walkway provides nice access to the steel bulkhead at the back portion of the inlet. On a moving tide a good rip current runs directly in front of this area. It is, as its motto states, "a great place to wet a line." You'll also find here a monument to the commercial and recreational fishermen, lobstermen, divers, and sailors from this area who lost their lives at sea.

You can catch all the species of fish mentioned in this text at either of these two locations along the inlet, but weakfish, fluke, and snapper blues are what most anglers seek here in spring and summer. Excellent parking is available on both sides of the inlet, but these spaces fill up quickly, especially in summertime. The parking is timed during the day on the Manasquan side and metered on the Point Pleasant side from April through October.

To get to the Point Pleasant side of the inlet take Route 35 South over the Manasquan River and make a left onto Broadway Drive. Go to the end, make a left, and you're there.

To get to the main channel of the Manasquan Inlet you can launch your boat from one of the many marinas located in the towns of Manasquan, Brielle, Point Pleasant, and Bricktown.

In summer the Manasquan Inlet is one of the busiest inlets in New Jersey.
Jim Freda photo.

MANASQUAN INLET
OVER THE RAIL

The rail at the Manasquan Inlet is one of the most easily accessible and fisherman-friendly places to fish in New Jersey. You can literally drive right up to the rail, park, and be fishing in a matter of minutes. On cold or rainy days you can sit in the car and watch folks pole for strikes while remaining warm and dry. It's also a great place for people who unable to walk out onto a jetty or across a beach but still want to enjoy some of the fine fishing our state has to offer.

All our main species of fish—stripers, blues, weakfish, albacore, fluke, and winter flounder—can be caught over the rail at the right time of year. But what has made this location so popular is the tremendous summer weakfish population that it harbors right along its edge.

Weakfish usually start to arrive in good numbers by the third or fourth week in May. During these first several weeks the largest fish of the season—the tiderunners, as they're called—provide anglers with a shot at a real trophy. These early-spring spawners are migrating through the inlet on their way to their spawning grounds in the estuary and the northern part of Barnegat Bay. Other fish also find the currents of the inlet as they move out from the backside of Barnegat Bay via the Point Pleasant Canal. The currents that run along the rail draw these fish in tight, making them easily accessible to anglers both young and old.

Two holes found along the rail are extremely productive during these weakfish runs. The first is located at its east end, right where the rail ties into the North Jetty of the Manasquan Inlet. The second is located at its west end, where the rail makes a 90-degree turn into what's referred to as Fisherman's Cove. The midsection of the rail also produces fish, but not of the quality or quantity of these two spots.

Both these holes are usually the first place that anglers set up. During the peak of a midsummer night's blitz it's not uncommon to find anglers shoulder to shoulder in both locations. Frustration levels can sometimes run high: Lines can easily become tangled if cooperation, teamwork, patience, and proper angling etiquette are not practiced. For the most part, however, you'll find many regulars returning night after night to share some good fishing and camaraderie. In fact, this location is home to some of the friendliest and most knowledgeable local fishermen around: the "Over the Rail Gang."

The most productive method for hooking into a good number of fish is to cast the 4- to 6-inch soft-bodied baits that have become so popular in recent years. The top producer for this location has been the Fin-S Fish in white, rainbow trout, olive and white, black and white, or pink. Bass Assassins or Sassy Shads rate a close second. And the old standby white bucktail will produce when all else fails. Trying to drift sandworms will be difficult and is better left for less crowded spots along the river.

Depending on the tide, different-weighted jigheads will be necessary to get your offering close enough to the bottom to draw strikes. A quarter ounce will work well when the tide is going slack, but you'll need an ounce or more when the tide is running. There's a quick drop-off only several yards in front of the rail, where the water depth can reach 15 feet.

The most productive tide by far is an incoming tide that begins to flow several hours before dusk and continues into the dark. Weakfish are nocturnal feeders, and any nighttime incoming tide in summer will turn them on. During this time you'll also find the boat traffic to be at a minimum. Weakfish can become very skittish and difficult to catch when there are a lot of boats around. This fishery remains consistent throughout the entire summer and ends sometime in early October.

The rail is one of the best locations along the Jersey shore to take kids fishing. The 4-foot high, four-railed structure provides ample safety for a child to fish against without danger of falling into the water. There are benches directly behind the rail where you can sit back and relax as baited poles hang in the water. And the numerous boats and commercial trawlers moving in and out of the inlet are always intriguing to watch.

For the kids you'll find abundant numbers of snappers here in late summer and early fall. Snappers are an excellent way to get a kid hooked on fishing. They're easy to catch and small enough for youngsters to reel in with no problem. To catch these baby bluefish, use enough a very small metal lure such as a Kastmaster or freshwater trout spinner.

Another option is to buy a snapper rig from a local bait shop. This rig features a small plastic tube fished ahead of a red and white wooden dowel. The dowel is quickly pulled across the top of the water, acting as an attractor as it splashes and gurgles along. You'll often see several snappers fighting over a plastic tube. Be careful when releasing these juvenile fish—they're fragile. Baby snappers are also great on the grill or in the frying pan, however.

If the rail is too crowded when the fishing is hot, you can move directly around the corner and fish in Fisherman's Cove. This area is wadable and offers a good alternative with plenty of available fish. Here you'll see the old bait shop that has now been taken over by the Monmouth County Parks System and converted into a Welcome Center. If you walk along the shoreline of the cove, you'll see a point about 1/4 mile to the west. Keep walking; this point is always worth investigating. Wading at this point will bring you close to the river's main channel. With a good cast using a spinning rod and a metal lure or jig, you can put your offering within striking range.

To get to the inlet rail follow Main Street in Manasquan east to its end and make a right onto First Avenue. Follow First Avenue to the end.

MANASQUAN RIVER
TRAIN BRIDGE/ROUTE 70 BRIDGE

The Manasquan River system is well known throughout central New Jersey as a top recreational location for boating, fishing, kayaking, and canoeing. It's also home to a large commercial fleet of draggers and netters, charter captains, and party boats, and it boasts one of New Jersey's largest offshore fleets of charter boats that target giant tuna. At its lower end you can find many popular restaurants and eateries that provide an excellent view of the water along with some fine casual dining. This "river island for wives"—so named by the early American Indians—is one of New Jersey's busiest river systems.

The entire river is approximately 18 miles long. Its upper section, above what's known as the narrows, is stocked with trout by the New Jersey Division of Fish and Game. Brown, rainbow, and brook trout are available for the freshwater angler. The lower section of the river is a typical marine estuary and hosts large populations of schoolie bass, weakfish, fluke, and winter flounder. Bluefish also frequent these waters but are much more transient.

The river's claim to fame is centered on its weakfish and fluke fishery. Starting in late May large tide-running weakfish enter the river to spawn in its tidal waters. In recent years weakfish of up to 12 pounds have been caught, with fish in the 6- to 8-pound range more the norm than the exception. Throughout the rest of the season smaller weakfish can be caught throughout the main channel, which runs from the train bridge west to the Route 70 Bridge. The fishery continues and extends into late fall, when larger weakies are once again caught.

The most popular method for catching weakfish in the Manasquan River is jigging Fin-S Fish. Many boaters take this approach because it's easy, clean, and effective. Fin-S Fish in pink, rainbow trout, or black/pearl colors in 4 1/2- to 5 1/2-inch lengths on 1/4- to 1/2-ounce leadheads are the favorites. If you're going to use plugs, small Bombers in the 4-inch range or Rat-L-Traps are the most effective. Later on in fall you can also live-line small snappers, peanut bunker, or spots. All three of these baitfish are apparently irresistible and will account for some of your largest weakfish.

Catching fluke, or flounder as they're called in South Jersey, is a favorite pastime for anglers of all ages and a great way to introduce a youngster to this wonderful sport of ours. This feisty flatfish is probably one of the best tasting of all the species mentioned in this text and makes for some fine table fare. You can easily limit out in the Manasquan River in a short period of time when the bite is on.

The preferred method for taking fluke is to use cut bait such as squid in combination with a killie, sand eel, or spearing. Many anglers elect to fish the baitfish alone, without the squid. Other baits that produce are sea robin and fluke belly. If you use the latter, keep in mind that the remaining carcass must still be above the legal minimum length.

When you're fishing for fluke, bigger bait usually produces bigger fish, possibly even what are referred to as doormats. A 6-pound or heavier fluke would fall into this category. Big baits include squid strips neatly trimmed into a triangular wedge at least 6 to 8 inches long and 1 to 1 1/2 inches wide. Smaller baits, however, will catch you a lot more fish, usually in the 2- to 3-pound range. Strip baits for these fish should be 1/2 inch wide and 4 inches long.

Targeting fluke in the river is a light-tackle sport. Spin or conventional gear loaded up with 6- to 8-pound test is all you need. Your hook should be a wide-gap English-style bait hook in size 1/0 or 2/0 or a size 10 Chestertown. A three-way swivel can be used to attach your leader and weight. A bank sinker will work fine, but make sure to use one heavy enough to bounce the bottom. When the fish are finicky, some anglers switch over to fishfinder rigs so the fluke can mouth the bait with the least amount of resistance.

Heavy boat traffic in the river, particularly on weekends, can shut off the fish. It's best either to get out early before the parade of boats starts heading for the inlet or to fish during the week. Make sure you bring a net and a cooler with ice to keep your catch fresh.

Some of the best action for weakfish or fluke is found along the edges of the boat channel that runs from the train bridge west to the Route 70 Bridge. As you near the Route 70 Bridge, the entrance to Point Pleasant Canal is also a hot spot. There are some deeper holes in the large eddy that forms at the mouth of the canal where its tidal flow pours into the river. In fall your best bet is to work the waters east of the train bridge into the inlet. This area is the final staging point for these fish before they move back into the ocean to begin their winter migrations.

Also look for a major cinderworm hatch that takes place in the back of the river in late spring and early summer. These 1- to 2-inch morsels are a favorite food of the resident schoolie bass population. During this time the bass can get very finicky, and catching them on the usual hardware or plugs can be difficult. This is when the fly rodder can score quite well by "matching the hatch" with small red and brown cinderworm patterns. Both floating and intermediate lines are effective. Just allow your fly to drift naturally with the current, giving it a slight twitch every few seconds.

Another significant event is a shrimp hatch in early spring. During flood tides, grass shrimp are sifted and pulled from the eelgrass and spartina beds that border the river. This really turns on the bass. If you're on the river at night, the familiar slurping and popping sounds of dining bass are easily heard. Once again the fly rodder has the edge here: Bob Popovics's Ultra Shrimp pattern is all you need. A floating line with an 8- to 9-foot leader is the way to go.

The New Jersey Division of Fish and Wildlife has undertaken an exciting new program to introduce a trophy sport fish—the sea-run brown trout—into the saltwater portion of the Manasquan River in the hope that a new fishery will develop. In October 1997, 16,065 eight-inch browns were stocked to begin the program. These fish are expected to return to the river after several years at sea at an average weight of 2 to 4 pounds. Subsequent stockings since 1997 have raised the total of sea-run browns to 110,645.

Several sea-run brown trout have been caught to date that have shown a significant increase in weight. There have been 11 confirmed catches of sea-run browns in fresh water and 5 in salt. On January 3, 2000, just upstream of the Garden State Parkway in Monmouth County, a sea-run brown weighing 7 pounds, 1 ounce, that was 23 inches long was caught by Paul Ripperger of Neptune City, New Jersey. Its clipped adipose fin indicated that it had been stocked in October 1997.

On November 12, 2000, a 5-pound sea-run brown trout was caught downstream of the Howell Golf Course. The fish measured 18 inches in length. The fin clip indicated that the division had stocked the fish in 1999. On November 30, 2000, a 9-pound sea-run brown was caught 1/2 mile upstream from Hospital Road. The fish measured 28 inches in length, as reported by the Division of Fish and Wildlife.

These trout look somewhat similar to their freshwater counterparts but have more of an overall silvery coloration that masks most of the spots on a brown trout's body. Numerous small spots remain on the head.

Anyone catching a sea-run brown is asked to report the catch to the Bureau of Freshwater Fisheries at either (908) 236-2118 or (609) 292-8642. The future success of this program depends on the number of fish caught and reported.

POINT PLEASANT CANAL

POINT PLEASANT HOSPITAL/ROUTE 88 BRIDGE/BRIDGE AVENUE BRIDGE/STATE POLICE BARRACKS/BAY AVENUE

Point Pleasant Canal, located in the western part of the Manasquan River estuary system, offers some unique fishing opportunities for both the shorebound angler and boat fishermen. This 2-mile-long man-made structure connects the northernmost portion of Barnegat Bay with the Manasquan River. This allows for the free flow of water—governed by tidal flows and variations—between these two systems. The Canal lies completely within the boundaries of Point Pleasant Borough and was originally called Bay Head–Manasquan Canal. Its name was changed in 1964.

The waters of the two systems successfully merged for the first time on December 15, 1925, and the Canal waters became navigable in 1926. The Canal provides safe passage for boaters who are heading south and looking to get away from the occasionally dangerous waters of the Atlantic. By turning west into the Manasquan Inlet and heading upriver for approximately 2 miles, you'll find the Canal's entrance on the south side of the river. Its entrance is bordered by the large brick Point Pleasant Hospital.

After its inception the canal was plagued with problems that hindered boaters trying to navigate these waters. Strong currents due to differences in tidal height around the Route 88 Bridge, one of two bridges that span the canal, created a series of rapids that made these waters treacherous. Many boaters were hopelessly caught in these currents and wrecked on the bridge. The Manasquan Inlet shoaled up and closed several months after the canal's opening; many believe this was caused by the diversion of the river water into the canal. The banks of the canal also became so seriously eroded that the Army Corps of Engineers put wooden bulkheads in place.

Today the Route 88 Bridge and Bridge Avenue (Lovelandtown) Bridge across the Canal have been replaced with two new lift bridges. The stone shelving beneath the old bridges has been removed so the treacherous rapids that existed around these structures are now gone. The wooden bulkheading along the length of the Canal has also been replaced with steel. The Canal's average depth is approximately 18 to 20 feet at mean low water. Its width is approximately 140 feet at its widest span.

The Canal offers some prime fishing opportunities throughout the season. Striped bass and weakfish are the predominant species targeted in this 2-mile stretch. However, at either end of its dual mouth the Canal is well known for the excellent winter flounder catches in April and good fluke catches during the summer.

You'll need to employ different tactics to fish the canal successfully. The first and foremost consideration to pay attention to is the tide. When the tide is ebbing or flowing the currents in the channel are extremely fast. It's next to impossible to get your bait or imitation down in the water column to hold in the strike zone. For this reason you'll need to concentrate your efforts on either side of the slack high or low tide.

The slack tide in the Canal will occur approximately three hours after it occurs along the oceanfront. Thus, when you try to calculate the time of slack tide from a local tide chart, you'll need to add on these hours. You'll have a window of about 30 to 40 minutes between tides when there's very little current; these are the best times to fish, and their timing will vary depending on the moon phase and wind direction. During the slack tide it's not uncommon to see and hear fish breaking on the surface as they come up to hammer the baits.

In summer and fall the boat traffic going through the Canal makes it very difficult to fish during the middle of the day. It's not a good idea to be drifting without power, since the wakes thrown by passing boats can quickly have you spinning in circles. Reserve your drifting for early in the morning or during the late-evening hours. Boat traffic also has a negative effect on the fish—it drives them down. Weakfish are extremely boat shy, so expect this action to be best when traffic is at a minimum.

The Canal is fished most effectively by boat, but the

shorebound angler can find access on either side of its banks. A footpath runs along parts of the east and west side of the Canal. There are three main spots where you'll usually find any number of fishermen during the season: the northern sections of the Canal around the Point Pleasant Hospital, the area near the Route 88 Bridge next to the Point Pleasant Fire Company, and the area on either side of the state police barracks just south of the Bridge Avenue Bridge, all accessible from the street. These areas provide enough room to fish comfortably and cast into the canal. Other areas along the Canal's length are inaccessible due to the homes that butt up against the bulkheads.

The area just south of the state police barracks on the west side is a New Jersey Department of Environmental Protection access site. It's located off Beach Boulevard and provides a good open area for casting into the canal. One of the Canal's public boat ramps is available here. If you like to fly fish, this spot is a good one, because you can stand along the bulkhead at the mouth of the launch ramp and cast into the canal with nothing impeding your backcast.

On the east side just south of the barracks you'll find a large parking area as you head down Mount Place off Bay Avenue. Here you can pull up and park right against the bulkhead and easily cast plugs or jigs, or fish live baits. A ledge with a quick drop-off lies directly in front of this area; casting parallel to the steel bulkhead and swimming your bait back along its edge is a very effective method of producing strikes. This drop-off is significant in that you can reach depths of up to 15 feet only several yards from the bulkhead.

Another very good access point for wading is found on the east side of the Canal at the end of Bay Avenue. Here you'll find another public boat launch that can handle small boats up to about 15 or 18 feet. This area is at the mouth of the canal where it dumps into Barnegat Bay. You can easily reach the channel from this point while casting spin or conventional gear. The water quickly drops to 20 feet deep here; there's also a nice dock to fish from. Public access is available in front of the town houses that line the Canal just to the right of this point. Average water depths along this area are in the 16- to 18-foot range.

Fishing the Canal by boat is the best method for covering its entire length. At times you'll find fish holding or breaking water in one particular section of the canal and not others; a boat can put you on these fish quickly. There are two times of year when boaters concentrate their efforts on drifting the canal. The first is in early spring—April and May. This is when herring invade the Canal, and the big bass are on them. Boaters live-line herring as they drift through the Canal and experience quite a thrill when one of these burly bass provides a spine-tingling runoff.

The second optimal time is in summer, when the Canal is invaded by weakfish that can easily be caught by jigging Fin-S Fish 4 to 7 inches long. White bucktails tipped with soft plastic trailers are also very effective for taking fish. Early-morning or evening hours are best. Other veteran anglers fish for the big bass that hold in the deeper waters around bridge abutments. This is also a late-night affair; the ticket to score is drifting live eels. Using an appropriate-sized egg sinker placed 3 to 4 feet above the eel will allow it to get close enough to the bottom while offering the least amount of resistance on the pickup. Use a barrel swivel to keep the sinker from sliding down the leader.

There are many access roads to get to the Point Pleasant Canal once you're in the borough. To find the boat ramp, take Route 35 South to Route 88 West. Head west down 88 to Bay Avenue and make a left. Go straight to Bridge Avenue and turn right, then go over the bridge and take the first left at the bottom. This is Rue Lido Drive. Make the first left onto Beach Boulevard and you'll see the launch ramp on your left.

Upper Barnegat Bay

BAY HEAD HARBOR/BEAVER DAM CREEK/METEDECONK RIVER/HERRING ISLAND/GUNNERS DITCH/MANTOLOKING BRIDGE/SWAN POINT NATURAL AREA

When most New Jersey anglers think of Barnegat Bay, they think of the inland waters that lie behind the Barnegat Inlet and "Old Barney," the Barnegat Lighthouse. This area, however, is only a small section of the 75-square-mile expanse that encompasses this lagoon-type estuarine system. Beginning at its northernmost boundary at the southern end of the Point Pleasant Canal, the bay system extends southward for nearly 35 miles to the southern end of the town of Barnegat. Here the bay waters merge with what's known as Manahawkin Bay and Little Egg Harbor.

Beaver Dam Creek, the Metedeconk River, the Edwin B. Forsythe Wildlife Refuge, and Swan Point State Natural Area border the upper part of the bay on its western boundary. To the east the towns of Bay Head and Mantoloking border the upper bay. Heavily fished, this area is an extremely productive part of the bay due to the tidal flows created by water moving into and out of the Point Pleasant Canal.

I'm fortunate enough to have benefited from the expertise of Darin Muly, a Shore Catch Guide who's a lifelong resident of this area and literally grew up on these waters. He provided me with the local knowledge of this area.

The upper Barnegat Bay is best known for weakfish and small schoolie bass. Winter and summer flounder are also prevalent during the season. As you enter the northernmost portion of the bay from the Point Pleasant Canal, you'll find the beginning of the Intracoastal Waterway (ICW). This area along Bay Head Harbor is a good ambush point for small stripers and weakfish as they trap the bait that washes out of the canal. Just east of the channel is a flat about 300 yards wide. The water depth in this area extends from 3 to 6 feet and can easily be drifted in a small boat. Darin says the best time to fish this area is at dusk with 4- to 5-inch Fin-S Fish on 1/4-ounce leadhead jig. Bubble gum and black and gold are two of his most popular and productive colors. Some rather large weakfish in the 9- to 10-pound range are taken here at the beginning of June each year.

As you travel south from this point, the channel tends to split. To the west you'll see the entrance to Beaver Dam Creek and the mouth of the Metedeconk River. The east side of the split remains the ICW. Between the two channels at this point is a very large, unnavigable flat: At high tide the water depth is only 2 to 4 feet, and running aground is a real threat. You need to stay in the channels as you move south along this area. This flat area can be extremely productive, however, on an incoming tide in the morning. Darin notes that weakfish will tend to move up into these shallows to feed. Maneuvering your boat along the edges and casting into the flats is an effective method that produces fish. As the sun rises into the sky, the fish drop back into the channel. The channel is about 50 yards wide and runs from 8 to 14 feet deep in some of its bigger holes.

As you move farther south, you'll come to Herring Island. This is federally protected land; you're not allowed to trespass or beach your boat here. It's very well marked and patrolled. West of the island, next to the Edwin B. Forsythe Refuge, is one of the best-known holes in northern Barnegat Bay: Gunners Ditch. Darin notes that Gunners Ditch is a well-known weakfish hole that drops off quickly from 3 feet of water to 14 feet. The passage here is narrow, just about 50 yards wide, and a strong current funnels through this area on the changing tides. On an incoming tide any bait on the flats gets washed through here.

Darin brought to my attention that Gunners Ditch got its name from the duck hunting that has long taken place in this area. As you move through, you'll see many duck blinds set up just off the point to the west. This is a very popular area to duck hunt; caution should be exercised during the hunting season, in November. If you're running to the ocean from the back part of the bay to cash in on November's hot striper action, it's highly recommended that you stay clear of any decoys you see in the water.

At the southern end of Herring Island, Gunners Ditch and the ICW merge. Darin points out that there's a nice hole here about 15 feet deep. The flats on either side go up to 4 feet. Definitely check out this spot before you move farther south.

Another location to check out in this area is the mouth of the Metedeconk River, northwest of Gunners Ditch. The channel mouths that empty into the Metedeconk are very productive along this stretch. One in particular that's worth checking out is at the entrance to the Metedeconk River Yacht Club. Here you'll find a 10-foot hole where weakfish like to hang out. This entire mouth is about 1/2 mile wide by 1/2 mile long and supports good populations of nice-sized weakies, schoolie bass, and small blues throughout the season.

Heading farther south will bring you to the Mantoloking Bridge, which runs from west to east across the bay. Either side of this relatively small bridge—north or south—is a great spot to fish. The water is shallower toward the eastern end of the bridge. Two small channels under the bridge are each about 15 feet deep. Jigging in this area is very productive from June through September for weakfish and small bass. You won't pull many big bass from here, but that's made up for by the numbers of bass you can catch. Nice-sized weakfish can also be taken. Release any short bass carefully, handling them as little as possible.

Just south of the Mantoloking Bridge is a red channel marker that brings you up to Swan Point, part of the Swan Point State Natural Area. Darin notes that there's a very nice hole just north of this marker. The hole is about 100 yards long by 50 yards wide with 15-foot water depths. It will very easily show up on your depth recorder. Once again, jigging the hole with Fin-S Fish is the preferred method. Darin recommends black and gold, bubble gum, and Arkansas shiner as the preferred colors. Also, keep your tackle on the light side.

There's good access on foot to the northern part of the bay just off Mantoloking Road as you head east toward the bridge. Make a left onto Tilton Road and head to the water. You can walk a 1/4-mile stretch of hard sand beach at this point. If you're a fly fisher, this is a great location to cast. As you walk east along these banks, you'll see some small creek outflows; these are very shallow with hard sand bottoms that turn to soft mud as you move into the marshes. Stay along the sand beach and don't venture toward the soft mud: It can be very dangerous.

To successfully fly fish any part of the northern bay, try an intermediate line. If you're fishing deeper holes while the tide is running, switch over to a 250- to 350-grain line to get your flies down deeper. In the early part of the season the water is usually muddy; brightly colored flies will draw attention. Six- and 7-weight rods with light tippets in the 8- to 10-pound class work just fine.

To get to the northern part of Barnegat Bay, head down Bridge Avenue in Point Pleasant until you come to Bay Avenue. Take Bay Avenue to the end; you'll see a public boat launch and the bay directly in front of you. There's limited trailer parking around the ramp on the streets adjacent to the town houses.

Eighteen to 24-foot center consoles, like Captain Gene Quigley's Parker of Shore Catch
Charters, are ideally suited for New Jersey's inshore waters.
Nick Curcione photo.

ISLAND BEACH STATE PARK

SHORT ROAD/MAINTENANCE SHED/GILLIKENS /BATHING BEACHES/AREAS 1–23

At the southern end of the central New Jersey coastline lies Island Beach State Park. This 9.5-mile stretch of barrier beach is a virtual paradise of undisturbed maritime wilderness overspread by rolling dunes, tidal marshes, lush vegetation, and diverse wildlife. The island is home to New Jersey's largest osprey population and serves as a sanctuary for many other species of waterfowl, migratory birds, and shorebirds.

Island Beach is actually the final part of the first section of barrier beach you encounter as you head north to south along our coastline. In its entirety this barrier island is 25 miles long and extends from the Manasquan Inlet south to the Barnegat Inlet. From 1740 to 1850 Island Beach was a true island: The now extinct Cranberry Inlet bordered its northern end. Since then this inlet has permanently closed.

The earliest fishermen on the island were the Lenape Indians. Later great explorers such as Henry Hudson investigated this bountiful resource and deemed it "a very good land." Very good indeed, for the island is today one of the most popular state parks in New Jersey with almost a million visitors a year. The Division of Parks and Forestry under the Department of Environmental Protection presently operates the park. The state purchased the island in 1953 for $2.7 million from the heirs of the Henry Phipps estate, the former owners.

During World War II the island played a key role as one of our nation's research and development testing facilities. A project code-named Operation Bumblebee saw the supersonic ram-jet rocket make its first successful flight in 1945.

The park opened for recreational activities in 1959. These include fishing, swimming, kayaking, picnicking, nature walking, and sunbathing. Long before this time, however, fishermen were operating beach buggies along the outer shores in search of trophy bass and bluefish. This ambience has remained, and has put Island Beach State Park at the top of the list of places for the serious angler to fish in New Jersey.

Besides the natural beauty that draws many fishermen to this location, the island is well known for consistently producing trophy fish. Big bass, alligator blues, reel-screeching albacore, tide-running weakies, and doormat fluke are the mainstay of the diverse species that can be found here. Add to this the ability to be mobile with a four-by-four sport utility vehicle along 9 miles of beach and you have by far the mecca of all surf-fishing locations in our state.

The island is divided into three management zones: the northern natural area, the central recreation zone, and the southern natural area. The northern zone is limited to ocean beach fishing only; the central zone has ocean and bay fishing, but ocean fishing is restricted during the summer, when this area becomes the park's bathing spot. The southern zone provides year-round access for ocean or bay fishing.

When you drive onto the island, you'll find limited parking in the northern zone. As soon as you enter you'll see Short Road on your left, where you can park and walk over the dune to the beach. Approximately .7 mile in there's a small area by a maintenance shed that will hold 12 cars. In the central zone there are two large parking lots that hold 900 and 950 cars, respectively. In the southern zone you'll find parking areas designated from area 1 to area 23 that have adequate parking.

The fishing season at the island begins in early April when striped bass and weakfish begin to invade the warmer backwaters of Barnegat Bay. Here you can wade the flats by accessing the backwaters from area 7 (Tices Shoal), area 15, or area 21. These are the most popular locations, but others hold fish as well. Area 10 is also worth investigating. All the areas are well marked and easy to locate. The roadway along the island runs straight; there's no chance that you'll get lost or miss a turn. These areas are also very popular for fishing from a kayak.

By May good numbers of bluefish have arrived on the flats, and the back bay waters come alive with fly fishermen. These areas are ideal for the long rodder to cast intermediate or floating lines with poppers, Clousers, Half-and-Halfs, Deceivers, or Jiggy Flies. Fish are more than willing to cooperate, and blitzes are common.

These flats are home to many members of the Atlantic Saltwater Flyrodders—the largest saltwater fly-fishing club in the state. In fact the club had its roots right in this area. One of the sport's most innovative and creative fly tiers, Bob Popovics, spearheaded the revitalization of saltwater fly fishing in New Jersey during the late 1980s. Bob's Seaside Park home was the hub of activity that brought professionals and amateurs together.

The island's claim to fame, however, is the excellent surf fishing and beach buggy access that it has to offer. An angler with a buggy permit can travel the island from end to end following the fish and bait as they move along the beach. Rather large bass and blues are common in the island's surf, with some years producing fish in the 40-pound class. Bass in the 20-pound range are a common sight on the island—they don't even turn a head when brought into local tackle shops to be weighed in.

The island's northern end is generally deeper than the southern and has more pronounced bowls, cuts, sandbars, and holes to attract and hold fish. Being able to read the soft structure and topography of the beach will be the key to your success when it comes to hooking into fish. One thing to look for is darker water surrounded by lighter water. This darker water is a deep hole and a good place to set up.

On any given day you'll see many surf fishermen lined up with three or four rods held in sand spikes along the beach. Clams are the bait of choice for many who seek the trophies that lurk in these waters. Fresh clams always work best, but when they're unavailable anglers opt for salted or frozen clams. The trick to hooking into a large bass is to use the entire clam on a baitholder-style hook. Use a piece of elastic thread to tie on the clam if the water is rough. You may need as much as 8 ounces of lead to hold in the island's sweeping currents. A high-low rig or bait-finder rig is the setup of choice.

A big event each fall is the Annual Governor's Surf Fishing Tournament. It's held the first Sunday of October and is one of the largest events of its kind on the East Coast. Several thousand anglers compete for the prestigious Governor's Cup for catching the longest eligible fish. The winner's name is engraved on the cup and placed on display in the lobby of the park office. There are many categories to enter and plenty of awards for the kids, too.

Fall is the most popular time to fish the island, because hordes of mullet, peanut bunker, spearing, and bay anchovies run along the beach as they move southward. The action can heat to a fevered pitch, and trophy fish can be had with regularity. The best way to score big is to fish a live mullet or peanut bunker. These baits can be netted or snagged and then cast out on a spinning or conventional setup using a small bait hook. Frozen mullet can also be fished on a mullet rig with a float to keep the bait away from the crabs. Bombers, Yozuris, Megabaits, or Danny-style plugs, along with Fin-S Fish and shad bodies, are also excellent choices. The key is to match the size and color of the plug or soft plastic body to the size and color of the bait. Top-

Fall is a prime time for bass and bluefish blitzes along the beach.
Shell E. Caris photo.

water Polaris-style poppers are also deadly and can give you quite a rush when a bass or blue is thrashing through the water in hot pursuit. Bass and bluefish blitzes are common at this time of year—and are one of the reasons why the island can get very crowded, especially on weekends. For this reason the park limits access to the first 500 vehicles that enter the island each day.

Once you pass the tollgate there are only three access points to get your beach buggy onto the beach. The first is 2.1 miles from the park's entrance and is called Gillikens. This is one of the most popular fishing areas on the island because of its deeper water and numerous holes. It consistently gives up big fish year after year. After this you will find access at area A-7, 4.9 miles in, and area A-23, 8.1 miles from the entrance. To operate a beach buggy you need a yearly permit ($125) or a three-day pass ($25). You'll also need to carry all the necessary safety equipment, which must be in compliance with the New Jersey Beach Buggy Association. (The NJBBA, founded at Island Beach State Park in 1954, is a nonprofit organization that fights for continued beach access for mobile sport-fishing vehicles.) It's highly recommended that you deflate your tires to 15 pounds before traveling on the sand. Deflating the tire increases the surface area that comes in contact with the sand. This reduces the downward pressure that the tire exerts on the sand; as a result, it doesn't dig in or bog down in the sand.

There are two air stations on the island where you can reinflate your tires. The first is located in the parking lot of the park headquarters, 3.6 miles from the tollgate; the second is at area 6, 4.8 miles from the tollgate.

When you're driving on the island, please be aware that the beach speed limit is 10 miles per hour. On the roadway you should be alert for bicyclists, animals (particularly foxes), and other small organisms.

BARNEGAT INLET
MAIN CHANNEL/SUNKEN JETTY/MEYERS HOLE/THE DYKE

Twenty-five miles south of the Manasquan Inlet is one of New Jersey's busiest inlets, Barnegat. This inlet separates Island Beach State Park to the north and Long Beach Island to the south. It serves as the primary access link between the Atlantic Ocean and Barnegat Bay.

The strong tidal flows that are associated with this inlet act as a magnet attracting stripers, blues, weakfish, and albacore to these waters. Abundant baits such as herring, menhaden, spearing, snappers, and bay anchovies are present throughout the season. To best describe this fishery I would be remiss if I didn't use the words *world class*. This inlet is where the serious boater can tangle with 50-pound-plus bass and teen-sized blues, weakfish, and albacore.

Early topographic maps dating back to the 1800s indicate that the Barnegat Inlet has migrated to the south over time. In 1940 two rubble-mound jetties were constructed as part of a federal navigation project to stabilize the inlet. The North Jetty was 4,900 feet long and the South Jetty was 2,950 feet long. The two were 3,500 feet apart at their landward ends, and converged to 1,000 feet apart at their seaward ends. This arrowhead design was an attempt to keep the inlet mouth from shoaling up.

Due to continued navigational problems in the inlet a new South Jetty was completed in 1991. This jetty is 4,270 feet long and parallels the North Jetty. The old South Jetty was not removed, but the region between the two was filled in.

When navigating the inlet today, you're still going to need caution, particularly during any storms or at times of heavy boat traffic. At the back section of the inlet near "Old Barney," the Barnegat Lighthouse, there exists a shoal that can quickly put you in trouble if you don't stay in the channel. The channel weaves its way completely across the inlet from south to north. The North Channel that runs along the North Jetty is the safest and most widely used channel for running the inlet. At the inlet's mouth in the northeast corner a series of shoals makes these waters unnavigable during times of high winds and rough seas. For this reason the inlet derived its name from the Dutch; it translates as "breakers inlet."

As you approach the end of the North Jetty, you'll notice that its last section is sunken. This was the original height of the North Jetty before it too was reconstructed. This section was never added to. It's invisible at high tide, and if you're unfamiliar with the area it'll give you the illusion that you can run into the inlet between the light tower and the tip of the North Jetty. Trying to do so will in fact result in disaster, because these jetty rocks lie just below the surface. At low tide they're clearly visible.

This area all around the sunken jetty—from the light tower landward to where it meets the exposed tip of the North Jetty—is the prime location for trophy stripers. Here's where an experienced boater will position his boat along its sides and cast into the sunken rocks, retrieving back toward the boat. Live-lining with a herring, bunker, or eel is the most effective method for hooking into a large striper. Each season several 50-pound bass are taken from this location, along with at least a dozen 40-pounders and numerous 30s and 20s.

Drifting along either side of the sunken jetty will take a good deal of boat-handling skills and is better left to the experienced captains and locals. It isn't recommended for a novice boater. The strong currents along the rocks can quickly suck you in and put you in a rather precarious position.

Fishing the inlet in early spring will bring large scores of bass, weakfish, and some of the season's first bluefish to net, but the inlet is also well known for the fantastic action it provides in fall. As the mullet and peanut bunker migrate to their southern destinations, they run right along the sides of the jetty, tracing a perfect picture of its profile. Here bass and blues will wait in ambush to pin baits to the rocks. Literally thousands will get trapped. You can witness an awesome display of Mother Nature's predator–prey relationship as the big bass explode on these baits.

Fall also brings false albacore, bonito, and Spanish mackerel as the calendar moves from the end of September into early

October. The area directly around the mouth of the inlet is likely to be one of the most consistent locations for taking these fish along the entire Jersey coast. All three of these pelagic speedsters will test any drag system you have. The albie, however, is the where the real sport lies: These fish can tip the scales in the mid-teen range.

The false albacore usually shows around the inlet after the sun has come over the horizon. These fish follow a cyclical feeding pattern as they move from the ocean into the inlet and back again. A large forage base of bay anchovies (rainfish) is usually present in fall, and the albies gorge themselves on these 1- to 2-inch delicacies. You'll want to scale down your artificials when targeting these fish. If you're trolling, small flies or feathers in root beer, blond, or white are consistent producers, as are small metals such as Krocodiles, Hopkins, Kastmasters, and Deadly Dicks. Albies usually like a faster troll—about 7 knots—and will hit the artificials right in the boat's prop wash.

At the back of the inlet two other areas are worth inspecting, both on the south side by the lighthouse. The first is the channel directly behind the lighthouse, and the second is Meyers Hole. The channel behind the lighthouse has an average depth of 20 feet and drops off to 40 feet at one point. Good-sized bass and blues can be jigged here, but the preferred method of local sharpies is to drift live herring or eels. The trick is to attach anywhere from 2 to 4 ounces of lead to get your bait to the bottom.

As you follow the channel behind the lighthouse, you'll come to Meyers Hole, one of the best-known spots in lower Barnegat Bay. Meyers Hole runs parallel to Long Beach Island; it's bordered to the north by a series of bars and shoals and to the west by a spit of land known as the Dyke. This location provides good shelter from the wind and has depths that vary from 10 to 20 feet.

Meyers Hole supports good populations of winter and summer flounder but is best known as a weakfish hot spot. The fact that the hole is situated at the base of the inlet allows changing tidal flows to flush this area with baits. Weakfish just sit in the hole, waiting for the bait to come to them. Jigged Fin-S Fish or bucktails tipped with squid or shedder crab will take their share of fish, but the most productive method is chumming with live shrimp. Anchor your boat, start a nice chum slick, and drift a live shrimp back through it. It won't be long before every drift produces a fish.

In early spring, April and May, you can expect some rather large tide-running weakfish to be taken from this location. In recent years we've been seeing weakfish in excess of 10 pounds making an appearance. These are trophy fish and will provide an excellent fight on lighter tackle. Their characteristic headshake when hooked is the telltale sign that you're into a nice weakie. In summer the hole becomes inundated with much smaller fish: Weakies then average from 1 to 3 pounds.

A final spot that's worth checking out when you're done fishing Meyers Hole is behind the Dyke along the sod banks. These banks hold bass and weakfish throughout the season. The channel along the edge of the sod banks runs to a depth of approximately 16 feet and is best fished on the incoming tide. The Honey Hole, as the locals know it, is the most productive spot along this channel.

To access the Barnegat Inlet you'll find a public boat launch at the north end of the town of Barnegat Light on 10th Street. This will put you directly in the bay near Meyers Hole.

BARNEGAT INLET: NORTH JETTY

POCKET/HUMP/TIP/BULKHEAD

Two of the most improved jetties along the Jersey coast are the North and South Jetties of the Barnegat Inlet. Located 25 miles south of the Manasquan Inlet, these jetties offer the land-locked angler great access to our ocean water. Of all the jetties that I've fished, these two have to be among the most productive and consistent for hooking into stripers, blues, weakfish, and false albacore.

The North Jetty gets the nod as the better of the two because of the lengthy access it provides on the ocean side. The South Jetty has only a small access area on its south side, but it can still be very productive.

The North Jetty is a jetty for all seasons. In spring anglers who live-line herring have been known to hook into trophy bass all along this extended rock pile. Plug fishermen and fly fisher-men also score well as the water warms into the upper 50s in late April and early May.

In summertime the North Jetty continues to hold bass but is also invaded with a good class of weakfish that are very aggressive, particularly at night. Blues have been known to crash these rocks at any time and are probably the most unpredictable of the four species in terms of when they show up. Still, when they do, these fish will hit a variety of offerings. The artificials most commonly thrown for them are top-water poppers and metal such as single-hook Hopkins with a white bucktail.

It's fall, however, when the North Jetty really shines and draws fishermen from the tristate area to do battle with big bruis-ing bass and reel-screeching false albacore. You'll see hordes of mullet and peanut bunker get pinned along the rocks as they desperately try to escape from these marauding predators.

The North Jetty can be divided into three sections: Starting from the beach end and working out, these are the pock-et, the hump, and the tip.

The tip is well known for producing large bass at any time of year. Live-lining eels, bunker, or herring can produce fish that top the 50-pound mark. Each season several bass of this size are landed here. What makes this spot so productive is the structure. The jetty continues outward from the tip for another 1/8 mile but is partially submerged. A lot of white water and turbulence are produced at this point as incoming waves wash over the rocks and the strong tidal flows of the adjacent inlet collide. This rough water disorients the bait, and bass move in for an easy meal.

Plug fishermen also score their share of big bass as they cast out over the submerged jetty and let their plugs swim cautiously over these rocks. Big Bombers, Danny- or Lefty-style swimmers, and the Gibbs Polaris top-water poppers and darters are very effective. Black, blue, or yellow-backed swimmers with white bellies are the colors of choice. For top water all-white or -yellow will draw strikes. The traditional white bucktail from 1 to 2 ounces tipped with a Twister Tail or pork rind will always produce fish.

Fishermen come from the tristate area to fish the famed North Jetty at the Barnegat Inlet. Big fish and electrifying blitzes are common .   Shell E. Caris photo.

Another proven and widely used artificial is a 6-inch soft paddle-tail shad body. These shads are placed on the appropriate weighted jighead ranging from 1 ounce to 2 1/2 ounces. If you use a smaller body—in the 4-inch range—then a 1/2- to 1-ounce head is appropriate. All-white is the number one producer, with black and pearl a close second.

You'll also find good action on the inlet side of the tip, because there's a deep hole right along the rocks. This hole is well known for producing good-sized weakfish throughout the summer. On an outgoing tide you can cast into the inlet and have the current drift your artificial to the edge of the submerged jetty. Weighted shad bodies or Fin-S Fish are effective on this side, too.

As you head out to the tip of the North Jetty, you'll find that the rocks are relatively easy to walk on—with the exception of a small break just before the tip. You'll still need to exercise good common sense, however, because the jetty washes over easily during times of rough water or moon tides. Each year a number of overzealous anglers have to be rescued from the tip by the Coast Guard.

The middle section of the North Jetty is known as the hump, so named because it has the highest elevation above the water. The hump marks the halfway point of the North Jetty. From this point out to the tip is a favorite location for fly rodders to position themselves in fall to hook into their prized quarry, the false albacore. These southern speedsters usually arrive at the beginning of September and remain in good numbers through October. The North Jetty then becomes a haven for fly fishers, with many traveling from as far away as New York, Pennsylvania, and Connecticut. The long rodders outnumber and outproduce spin fishermen when the albies are around.

To hook into a false albacore on a fly rod is an experience you'll never forget. These pelagic speedsters can quickly strip 200 yards of line in a reel-screeching, arm-wrenching, lightning-fast run. Add to this the visual component of being able to see your quarry before the strike and your adrenaline will surge to a boil. The initial run of an albie will no doubt take you deep into your backing. Commonly referred to as "little tunnies," there's nothing diminutive about them when it comes to robust fighting ability.

Albies feed on a variety of baits but prefer small baits like bay anchovies, spearing, sand eels, and peanut bunker. To imitate these, your flies should be on the small side and dressed with white bellies and some flash. Green, blue, gray, blond, white, root beer, and even purple body colors are effective. Bob Popovics's Surf Candies are a favorite, along with Clousers, coneheads, glitter-head epoxies, small Crease Flies, and Bunny Flies. All will produce fish. If larger baits are present, size your fly accordingly.

False albacore have bloodred inedible meat, so it's best to land them quickly rather than playing them to exhaustion. This will increase their chance of survival. For this reason the fly fisher should break out the 11-weight rods and large-arbor reels to help deliver enough power and leverage for the task. Your typical false albacore will average in the 3- to 7-pound class, although teen-sized fish are caught each season along these rocks.

The pocket is the most landward part of the jetty, where the ocean beach and water meet. It's shallow but has good water movement in the form of rip currents that run along the sides of the rocks. In fall the pocket can be explosive as mullet and peanut bunker get pinned in this area by bass and blues. The water can erupt at times as these baits are aerialized. The pocket also holds a good summer population of fluke that can be caught on the traditional squid strips and killies. Fluke belly is another favorite bait here that always produces fish.

The pocket can be effectively fished from the rocks or the beach. Most of the time you'll see many-baited spike rods lined up along the beach. This is a favorite gathering place for owners of RVs and camper tops. On a typical summer or fall weekend there can be as many as 75 of these vehicles parked in the area.

Many seasoned anglers fish the North Jetty. One in particular whom you'll find long rodding on its rocks is Bob Popovics, well known across the country as one of the most innovative and creative fly tiers in the industry. He's been fishing these rocks for more than 30 years. He recommends never venturing out on these rocks without Korkers, particularly if you're unfamiliar with the area. For the fly fisherman he also recommends a good-quality stripping basket with large holes for drainage in case you take some wave splash—which is common.

Bob recommends a 10- or 11-weight rod with an intermediate- or slow-sinking line for fly fishing the North Jetty. The leader setup he uses is simple—usually just a straight piece of 20-pound monofilament. For sinking lines this is 3 to 4 feet in length, or up to 7 feet for use with intermediate lines. When it really gets nasty on the rocks, Bob recommends going to a 30-pound-test leader. This will allow you to lift a fish up onto the rocks without having to climb down and risk being swept off by a wave. The fish are not leader shy when the water is rough.

If it's too rough to fish on the ocean side, there's a very popular bulkhead located at the back of the North Jetty as you walk toward the bay. This is a prime spot for weakfish throughout the season and definitely worth checking out.

To access the North Jetty you'll need to drive to the end of Island Beach State Park, to area 23. From here you can drive along the beach if you have a permit or park and walk the remaining distance. If you're planning on walking, travel light, because it's a 1.4-mile hike along the beach.

LOWER BARNEGAT BAY

FORKED RIVER/BB BUOY/OYSTER CREEK CHANNEL /BI BUOY/DOUBLE CREEK CHANNEL/42 BUOY/SOD BANKS

Barnegat Bay is rich in maritime history dating as far back as Henry Hudson, who described it as a "great lake of water" in 1609. During the Revolutionary War early settlers used the extensive array of shoals, creeks, and channels to effectively out-maneuver British soldiers as they pirated and attacked ships sailing along the coast.

The diversity of ecological habitats and wildlife found in the bay makes it an integral part of the marine ecosystem in central New Jersey. The bay serves as a spawning and nursery grounds for a wide variety of fish, crustaceans, and birds. The abundance of marshes, cedar swamps, and other vegetation acts as a natural barrier against damaging floods and pollution.

A small boat is all you need to effectively fish Barnegat Bay, but caution needs to be exercised: Fast-approaching storms or squalls can quickly turn its placid waters into engulfing swells. Windblown water cresting across its shallow shoals can easily capsize even the most experienced captain. But on calm days the small-boater can target the shallow flats, whereas the larger boats will be restricted to the deeper channels. The bay's average water depth is 6 feet; it's approximately 5 miles across at its widest point as the crow flies.

In the lower bay there are many areas to search out any of the fish mentioned in this text. Probably the most abundant and easiest fish to catch, however, is the weakfish. From early April through late fall weakfish can be caught in a variety of locations using varying techniques. On days when the bite is on you can expect to hook a fish on every cast or drift.

Every boater who fishes the lower bay is familiar with the chain of buoys that mark the Intracoastal Waterway. Traveling from north to south along the western bay shore these buoys are the BB, BI, and 42. The BB Buoy marks the entrance to the Forked River, the BI Buoy marks the entrance to the Oyster Creek Channel, and the 42 Buoy marks the Double Creek Channel. All three buoys are located in water that averages 8 to 10 feet in depth. They're all well known as excellent locations to target weakfish from early spring right on through August.

A familiar sight on the waters of the lower bay is Captain Gene Quigley of Shore Catch Charters. Captain Gene has more than 20 years of fishing experience and is one of the bay's resident experts when it comes to locating and hooking into fish. I am extremely fortunate to have such a knowledgeable veteran as one of my partners in Shore Catch Guide Service. Captain Gene gave me the personal tour of his top-producing spots and helped me with the following information.

Captain Gene notes that the BI Buoy is probably the first location to produce weakfish, stripers, and blues in early spring, because of the warm-water discharge in this area from GPU's Oyster Creek Nuclear Power Plant. When the plant is discharging, the waters in the immediate vicinity of Oyster Creek climb into the upper-50- to low-60-degree range. When you consider that in early April the rest of the bay's temperatures are in the mid-40s, you can see why this area acts as a magnet for bait and fish. It's a good idea to thoroughly work over the area from the BI Buoy to the mouth of Oyster Creek when your boat first hits the water to begin a new season. This area can also be fished from shore, but you'll definitely need a guide to show you how to get back to the creek mouth.

The BB Buoy and the 42 Buoy are also consistent early-spring producers of weakfish and blues. Both are fished using the same methods, but Captain Gene mentions that the 42 Buoy is best fished from about 300 yards from shore right into the Double Creek Channel. A well-known landmark is the green Blind Camp on shore.

The Oyster Creek Channel is another favorite location where local charter captains and guides find consistent action throughout the season. This channel is also a favorite of anglers who want to target winter or summer flounder. Most of the fish will be picked up as you drift across the channel and come up on its ledges or drop-offs.

Oyster Creek Channel will take you from the western bayshore to the southern side of the Barnegat Inlet as you head out to the ocean. As you approach the lighthouse, you'll see the town of Barnegat Light. The channel is well marked but very narrow. It makes many dogleg turns as it weaves its way through the eelgrass flats and shoals. Trying to run a straight course across the bay to the inlet will result in running aground. Finding the few cuts that exist through the shoals is better left to the locals. Stay in the marked channel for safety reasons. As low tide approaches, the channel is easily identifiable by the darker-colored water that lies between lighter-shaded water on either side.

On your way out to the inlet the channel will bring you to one of the most famed locations in Barnegat Bay for big fish. This area is known as the sod banks or sedges and consistently produces trophy bass and weakfish throughout the season. The sod banks are easily identifiable by the extensive, low-lying array of eelgrass beds that blanket the area. A good landmark as you approach the western end of the sod banks is an old bait shack that still sits on the sedges.

As the channel runs along these sedge banks, you'll find an average depth of 18 to 20 feet with good tidal flows, steep drop-offs, and ledges. Directly across from the 40 Buoy you'll find what's known as Horsefoot—the first hole that Captain Gene recommends fishing. After thoroughly working this area, move to the other creek mouths that empty into the channel.

To hook into a trophy fish here, the preferred method is fishing bait. Drifting along the banks while live-lining herring during the day or eels at night will account for the biggest fish. Due to the strong tidal flows, though, you'll have to add an appropriate amount of weight above the herring or eel to get it down near the bottom. Another effective method is to anchor your boat in the channel and fish clams on the bottom while chumming. This method does interfere with the live-liners who are trying to drift through the channel, however.

Captain Gene notes that when the tide is ripping along the sod banks, it's important to point the bow of your boat into the current and throttle down to the appropriate rpms to hold relatively stationary. This will ensure that you have ample time to fish an area thoroughly without drifting past it too quickly.

Other productive methods in this area include fly fishing and jigging with artificials. The most productive jigs, according to Captain Gene, are the 6-inch shad bodies in all-white on 1- to 1 1/2- ounce heads. For weakfish bubble gum, albino, pink, rainbow trout, and natural-colored Fin-S Fish in the 4- to 5-inch range are all effective.

If the fly rod is your weapon of choice, you'll need 450- to 650-grain lines to get down into the strike zone. Many different flies will work, but you can always count on Bob Popovics's Jiggy Flies to put you into fish. The slender profile of this fly nicely simulates the abundant 6-inch spearing. Captain Gene feels that chartreuse and white or yellow and white are the best producers.

When retrieving your artificials, keep in mind that the majority of your strikes will occur as your offering starts to come up onto the ledges. Here bass and weaks use the sloping topography to their advantage as they pin bait against its sides.

To access the lower bay you can enter from the western creeks or rivers such as the Forked River, Oyster Creek, Double Creek, Cedar Creek, or Silver Bay. The other option is to enter from the ocean side through the Barnegat Inlet.

BARNEGAT LIGHT
BARNEGAT LIGHTHOUSE ROCKS/
SOUTH JETTY/BARNEGAT BAR

At the northern end of Long Beach Island is one of New Jersey's most famous and frequently visited landmarks—the Barnegat Lighthouse. Surrounded by maritime woodland of mostly red cedar and pitch pine, Barnegat Lighthouse State Park serves as a good starting point to access the South Jetty of the Barnegat Inlet.

The South Jetty is a focal point for anglers looking to cash in on some first-class action. When fishing this spot, you can't help but be in awe of Old Barney. The close proximity of this picturesque 175-foot-tall red and white wonder is a reminder of the captivating beauty that the New Jersey coast has to offer. Trophy bass and Kodak moments go hand in hand here.

The South Jetty was renovated and completed in 1991. This jetty is 4,270 feet long, with a flat top and a handrail for the first 1,000 feet around lighthouse. Striped bass are the South Jetty's claim to fame, and anglers who venture out to its tip are usually well prepared to do battle with some rather large linesiders. The trip out to the tip isn't easy, however. It's a rather long walk along the rocks starting from the lighthouse or across the dunes if you approach from the Barnegat Light beaches.

For this reason many anglers opt to fish around the lighthouse itself. There's good access along the jetty rocks along with a smaller fishable jetty that juts out behind the lighthouse. Extending even farther back, you'll find a bulkhead within casting distance of the channel. This area is also known as a great weakfish location; these fish can be found in the currents that sweep around the lighthouse's tip. Many fish pass through this point as they head into Meyers Hole in Barnegat Bay for the duration of the summer.

Besides being an excellent location to target bass, the tip of the South Jetty also gives anglers an ideal vantage point to target false albacore, bonito, and Spanish mackerel in fall. The length of this jetty is the key: As with the North Jetty, when the southern speedsters move around the tips of the rock piles and into the inlet, you're right there in the heat of the action.

Another point of interest that was brought to my attention by my partner and local expert Shell E. Caris has to due with the mass exodus of finger mullet from the backwaters of Barnegat Bay. As these baitfish make their exodus in fall, they run the rocks on the south side of the inlet. This puts the bait and busting fish right at your feet. Shell E. points out that many anglers miss cashing in on this action because they spend most of their time on the North Jetty.

When fishing the South Jetty, skipping a Gibbs Polaris popper in white across the top of the water can be deadly. The white underbelly of this surface plug is what the bass sees when it looks up at its prey from below. This matches the belly of the mullet, and the bass can't tell the difference between the real thing and the artificial. Things can really get into a frenzy during blitz conditions when stripers aren't in the mood to closely inspect baits, picking and choosing a particular one.

It's also a good idea to work the sides of the bait pods rather than casting directly into the busting fish: You'll find many bigger bass hanging outside the main body of fish. These lunkers avoid the heat of competition from the smaller fish by cunningly picking up the pieces or injured that are left behind. A good tactic in this situation is to throw a much larger swimming plug into the area and slowly work it across the surface. Big bass have been known to really slam this intruder as it moves in on their space. Atom and Danny swimmers or some of the custom wood swimmers, such as Lefty's, that many veteran anglers have stashed away are excellent choices.

Shell E. also recommends investigating the area where the old submerged South Jetty lies. This old jetty runs at an angle from the beach in Barnegat Light toward the new South Jetty. If you're walking out on the new jetty, you'll be parallel to the old jetty when you're about 50 feet from the tip. On the south side of the new jetty a pocket sometimes develops at this point; its size depends on the prevailing winds and number of storms that strike the coast. At times this area gets filled in with sand, and fishing it grows difficult. When the pocket is present, however, the underlying structure attracts good numbers of baitfish, which pull in the bigger fish.

At the northern end of the island, the Barnegat Bar is another very productive area. These ever-shifting shoals of sand begin off the tip of the South Jetty and extend southward to about 20th Street in Barnegat Light. The bar extends out from the beach for up to 1/2 mile in certain areas. At low tide the average depth on the bar ranges from 4 to 6 feet; it can be a rather treacherous location for a boater when the ocean is riled up. This area is better left to the locals and more experienced fishermen.

Barnegat Bar is productive because of its shallow water, which works to the benefit of predators: The places where baitfish would normally relocate, either up or down in the water column, are gone. Stripers, blues, weakfish, and fluke can regularly be caught here. Don't be surprised if you see a contingent of local anglers in full wet suits wading out onto the bar surf casting.

If you're a fly fisher, the backside of Barnegat Light—known as the Dyke—offers good access to Barnegat Bay. As you look to the northwest from behind the lighthouse, the Dyke is the strip of sand jutting out adjacent to Meyers Hole. Walking its banks is productive for stripers and weakfish, particularly in spring when these fish begin to move into Double Creek Channel. Access is found by making a left at the first yellow caution light at 20th Street and Central Avenue in Barnegat Light. You'll enter into the community of High Bar Harbor. Take your first right onto Arnold Boulevard, then the next right onto Sunset Boulevard. Travel to the end of the road and you'll see a path that takes you over the dune and onto the Dyke.

To get to the South Jetty at the lighthouse, take exit 63 off the Garden State Parkway and head east on Route 72 over the causeway into Ship Bottom. Make a left onto Long Beach Boulevard and follow this road north to the end of the island into the town of Barnegat Light. There you'll see the Barnegat Lighthouse State Park parking lot.

If you plan to fish the jetty at night, the lighthouse parking lot closes at 10 P.M. You'll need to find other parking if you're going to be out later than this—which can be difficult outside the park. Your other option is to park in Barnegat Light between Fourth and Eighth Streets and walk across the beach to the jetty.

Back bay flats, creek mouths, and river mouths are all early season hot spots you should target. Shore Catch guide, Darin Muly displays a nice weakie. Jim Freda photo.

LONG BEACH ISLAND

MANAHAWKIN BAY/BEACH HAVEN PUBLIC BULKHEAD/SOUTH JETTY

Just south of the Barnegat Inlet is the second barrier island that protects the coastline of New Jersey: Long Beach Island. LBI, as it's referred to, extends approximately 20 miles and ends at the Little Egg Inlet to its south.

In the days of early maritime history it's believed that Long Beach Island served as an ambush point for marauding pirates who would pillage and plunder passing cargo ships in the night. Promoted in the early 1900s as the island that was "six miles at sea," LBI quickly became a favorite vacation spot and hideaway for shore lovers. This signature distance referred to the sailing distance from the mainland town of Tuckerton across the tidal marshes to Beach Haven. In actuality it's closer to 5 miles.

The South Jetty of the Barnegat Inlet and the town of Barnegat Light border the northern end of the island. Here you'll also find "Old Barney," one of New Jersey's most famous lighthouses, overlooking the treacherous shoals just east of this skinny stretch of sand. At the southernmost end of the island are Holgate and the submerged bars of what remains of Tuckers Island.

After you exit the parkway, you'll need to travel east for 6 miles to go over the causeway that spans Manahawkin Bay. When you first reach the island you'll be in the borough of Ship Bottom. Heading south will take you into Brant Beach, Beach Haven, and finally Holgate; north from Ship Bottom, you'll enter Surf City, North Beach, Harvey Cedars, Loveladies, and finally Barnegat Light. The central and southern part of the island is where you'll find the many fine restaurants, eateries, shops, and amusement rides that make LBI a great family vacation spot at the Jersey shore.

As you ride along the island, you can't help but wonder what would happen if a hurricane made landfall here. At certain points the distance between the bay and the mighty Atlantic is less than 1/4 mile. The Great Storm of '62, which almost devastated the island, is one many islanders will never forget.

One of the unique features of LBI is that you can park at the end of almost any road and find good access to fishing on the bay side. In Beach Haven the borough has made it illegal to dock a boat at these access points and has placed benches for you to relax while fishing. You'll also find a public bulkhead located at the end of Dock Street as soon as you enter Beach Haven. This is an excellent place to take the kids to fish or crab. The wooden rail and bulkhead are well designed for safety. There are public rest rooms available, and a fish-cleaning table is provided. The channel is deep enough to catch fluke, weakfish, and plenty of snappers.

When visiting and fishing LBI I had the pleasure of meeting with Bruce Hoagland of Bruce and Pat's Bait and Tackle Shop in Surf City. Bruce is well known to everyone on the island as a local expert. He has been fishing here for more than 30 years and provided me with a wealth of information on its fishery.

Bruce notes that LBI consists of four broad areas, each with a distinct topographic profile. The first area extends along the beach from the northern end of the island at the Barnegat Light Bar to 20th Street in Barnegat Light. The next area extends along the beach from here to the end of Beach Haven. The third area is Holgate, and the fourth is the back bay side.

An interesting feature of LBI is that south of the Barnegat Inlet, the coastline turns inward. This change in the lay of the land may affect the migration route fish take as they move southward. Fish stay farther off the beach at the island's northern end as they follow the straight-line route they've been on. They do tend to come in and find the beach once again in the area of Harvey Cedars.

Bruce mentions that the typical beach profile is pretty much the same for the island's entire length. You'll find a short jetty about every four blocks (with the exception of Holgate, whose jetties are usually covered at high tide). An inner slough runs along the beach, then an outer bar. The slough can be as deep as 10 feet at high tide and shallow enough during low tides in some places to wade out to the outer bar. The norm here, however, is short casts: The fish and bait are both in the inner slough.

Bruce stresses that there are no secret or consistent spots on the island. One day one area along the beach may be productive, and the next day another. But he adds that the fishing on the first day of a northeast storm is always best along the beach. After a storm the sands shift, so look for spots where new cuts in the outer bar have opened up.

The island's bay side also offers ample fishing opportunities and should not be overlooked. Here three bays—Barnegat Bay, Manahawkin Bay, and Little Egg Harbor Bay—merge together. Any of the channels, deeper holes, or depressions here is an excellent location for bass, weakfish, fluke, and winter flounder. Some of the old dredge holes where sand was removed after the '62 storm still remain and are excellent starting points. Plenty of small bluefish are also available from spring through fall. The channels located underneath the four bridges as you come over the causeway onto the island are also popular and productive. Note that a local population of bass spawns in the backwaters that lead to estuary. These fish are present year-round.

One of the most interesting parts of my discussion with Bruce centered on the bait migrations along the New Jersey coast. As all savvy fishermen know, congregating and migrating bait acts as the stimulus to send bass, blues, and weaks into feeding frenzies. The result is a typical blitz that sends anglers running to the surf.

Most anglers associate these bait movements with dropping water temperatures, but Bruce believes the stimulus driving baits from back bay waters is the full moons that occur from August through November, which act as an innate calendar moving the baits. Around the time of the August full moon spearing will migrate out onto the beach. This is followed by the mullet migration near the time of September's full moon, and continues with the peanut bunker migration near the October and November full moons.

Bruce also notes that two bluefish populations inhabit New Jersey waters: a northern race and a southern race. The northern race spawns offshore after the July full moon; the southern race spawns off Hatteras, North Carolina, with the April full moon. You'll see the northern baby snappers in our bays in fall, when they're 3 to 5 inches long; the southern baby snappers, being older, are 10 to 12 inches long.

Staggering the bluefish spawn in this manner is Mother Nature's way of ensuring the survival of the species. For example, if it happens to be a cold spring and a large number of southern individuals don't survive, the northern spawn populations can propagate the species that year. The northern spawn occurs much later, so these fish would be unaffected by the unfavorable spring conditions. Thus the bluefish population remains intact.

Beach buggy access is available on LBI between Loveladies and Holgate. Access is closed in most boroughs from Memorial Day through Labor Day. Check with each borough or township for the exact dates and access points.

Plenty of beach buggy access is available from Brick Beach south to Cape May.
Jim Freda photo.

HOLGATE
POCKET/TIP/TUCKERS ISLAND

All along the Jersey coast Mother Nature's dynamic forces are constantly at work reshaping our beaches. The natural processes of erosion versus deposition of sand are at work together, either cutting away at our beaches or building them up. Among the factors affecting these processes are wave heights, particularly during nor'easters or hurricanes—the times when the most drastic reshaping of our coastline takes place.

Over the past several centuries the southern end of Long Beach Island has been as thoroughly reshaped as any spot in the state. Originally known as Tuckers Beach, this section of coastline has seen the now impassable Beach Haven Inlet opened and closed many times through the years. At some points it has become bermed up enough to connect with the former Tuckers Island, just to the south, a quiet but popular resort where beachgoers could enjoy cool seashore breezes and good fishing and hunting. Unfortunately, in 1929 the entire island was wiped off the charts by a devastating nor'easter. All that remains today are the dangerous shoals that make navigating along the inlet shores of Holgate extremely treacherous. It's hard to believe that in colonial times the inlet was 2 miles wide and served as a major entry port for ships heading into Fishtown (now known as Tuckerton).

Today the Holgate section of Long Beach Island is still subjected to the powerful forces of Mother Nature and remains in its natural dune state as in centuries past. There are more than 400 acres of barrier beach, dunes, and tidal salt marshes. The entire area is designated the Edwin B. Forsythe National Wildlife Refuge and is the only section of LBI without jetties. Locals know it as a place to read the beach—to put all their knowledge and experience together to pick out the cuts, rips, sloughs, and bars. There are no measuring scales or bragging rights here, just true solitude for a fisherman to do what he likes best.

This section of beach at the end of the island stretches

about 2 1/2 miles. You can walk to the southernmost tip, but it's definitely a hike. The majority of the anglers fishing this section have a beach buggy permit from Long Beach Township. This permit costs $50 and can be obtained at the police station at 68th Street and Long Beach Boulevard.

Beach access is closed, however, from April until sometime in September to protect migrating birds. It reopens when bird nesting is over. Sometimes the northern two-thirds of Holgate reopens toward the end of August and the tip reopens later. Holgate is an important area for nesting piping plovers, least terns, and black skimmers, all three listed by the state of New Jersey as endangered. The piping plover is also listed by the federal government as threatened along the entire East Coast. As many as 50 other bird species also nest at Holgate in spring and summer.

A parking lot at the entrance to Holgate offers parking for approximately 60 cars. Right at the beginning of the refuge there's a bulkhead and small rock jetty. The island turns inward at this point, and a nice bowl has developed here. From this vantage point it's easy to see that the littoral drift along the island runs from north to south. This area can be loaded with bait in fall and makes a good point to investigate first. Because of its close proximity to the parking area, it can get crowded early.

Throwing a cast net along an open beach is an excellent way to capture live baits during their coastal migration. Bob Popovics photo.

READING THE WATER

Along many of New Jersey's beaches you can't help but be captured by the Atlantic's breathtaking beauty and titanic vastness. If you're a beginning surf caster, though, you're also going to be wondering where in this broad expanse of water you should spend your time casting and seeking your prey. Learning how to read the water is crucial to saltwater fishing.

Beaches are dynamic in nature, changing all the time, growing and eroding as part of their natural cycle. What you see one day may or may not be there the next. A deep hole perfectly situated between two bars and full of fish might fill in overnight as a result of strong wave action. If beaches were stagnant and never changed there would be topographic maps available showing their permanent profiles. Such is not the case.

Instead you must look for clues as to where the most productive areas are. Along the New Jersey coast these visual clues are for the most part the same everywhere. Learning what they are will allow you to go to a totally unfamiliar beach and fish it with the confidence that you're in the right place.

As I noted, whether a beach grows or erodes is determined largely by the wave heights that strike it. During our winters the dominant wave type is what's called a plunging breaker, which is characterized by the tube that attracts surfers. Plunging breakers pull sand from a beach and cause it to erode. In summer, however, the dominant wave type is the spilling breaker, which doesn't form a tube. Instead, when it breaks the top of the wave simply spills over and gently rolls toward the beach. Spilling breakers push sand toward a beach, causing it to grow. Over time, whether a beach grows or erodes will be determined by whether the rate of deposition exceeds the rate of erosion or vice versa.

As a result of these waves types you'll find that springtime offers the most diversity in beach topography. Look for the formation of extensive sandbars in the surf zone just off the beach. These sandbars will be parallel to the shoreline. To identify their exact location, scout out the beach that you're going to fish at dead low tide, when some of these bars will be exposed. Or you can watch how the waves are breaking as they approach the beach. A wave will break when it starts to feel the bottom. Therefore, as a wave rolls over a bar it should begin to crest. Use these cresting waves to pinpoint the location of the bar.

Sandbars have drop-offs located in front of them (toward the beach) and directly behind them. At high tides fish will come over a bar into the deeper water in front of it. The area is referred to as a slough or, in some areas, a trough, and it puts fish right at your feet. Sloughs can run for many miles along the beach. They're ideal ambush points for predators, because the bait is for the most part trapped between two walls of sand, the bar and the beach.

Sandbars are also interspersed with deep holes or cuts along their lengths. These are formed when strong rip currents extending from the beach break through a bar and gouge it out. These rips and cuts are two of the best places to begin casting.

To spot a hole or cut, look for a deeper or darker coloration of the water surrounded on both sides by a lighter greenish hue. Using polarized sunglasses will greatly enhance your ability to read the water and see these sometimes subtle differences. These lenses eliminate surface glare and allow you to see into the water.

To identify a rip, look for water moving or being pulled away from the beach. As the rip pulls out, look for it to churn up sand from the bottom, particularly if it has been supplied by an energetic backwash from a sloping beach face. The churned-up sand will cause the area of the rip to become lighter in color than the water on either side of it.

Remember that the topographic profile visible on the beach extends into the water. Points are spits of sand that jut out in the water. Bowls are indents in the shoreline, usually located between two points. Both areas attract bait and fish.

Reading the water is a skill that you'll develop over time. Once it's acquired, each new beach that you visit to fish will look like a jigsaw puzzle with many pieces—but now you'll know where all the pieces fit.

An event that gets a lot of attention here is the Annual Long Beach Island Surf Fishing Tournament, sponsored by the Ocean County Chamber of Commerce. It's one of the oldest surf-fishing tournaments in the state—approaching its 50th year. This six-week tournament runs from the second week in October to the third week in November. The targeted species are striped bass and bluefish. Fishing is allowed from the beach, jetties, inlet, and bay. No boat-caught fish are allowed. Grand, segment, weekend, weekly, and daily cash prizes are awarded, and there's even a very lucrative cash prize for an angler lucky enough to break the state bluefish record.

At the southern end of the island you can find beach access points at Nelson Avenue, Scott Avenue, Harding Avenue, and Washington Avenue.

Hiring a surf guide or charter captain is an excellent way to learn how to read the water to locate fish. Here Alan Sandfelt is all smiles as he teams up with the author.
Jim Freda photo.

LITTLE EGG INLET

BEACH HAVEN INLET/
OLD COAST GUARD STATION/
SHOOTING THOROUGHFARE/GRASSY CHANNEL

Heading south to the end of Long Beach Island, you'll encounter a pair of unimproved inlets, without jetties. Existing in their natural states, the Beach Haven Inlet and Little Egg Inlet are notorious for their shifting sands. The nearly 2-mile-wide waterway between Holgate and Pullen Island to the south is in a constant state of flux. Strong northeast storms over the last several hundred years have shifted shoals, leading to numerous shipwrecks by inexperienced navigators.

Charts that date back as far as the late 1600s show that these two inlets have periodically merged and then split apart again. In 1903 it was recorded that the two inlets had joined into what was called the New Inlet at the time. But as Mother Nature would have it, an unimaginable northeast blizzard in February 1920 spilt them again. The Beach Haven Inlet continued to migrate to the south, approaching the former Sea Haven Resort and Little Egg Harbor Lighthouse on Tuckers Island. In 1927 the island and lighthouse were washed away.

Today the Coast Guard has officially closed the Beach Haven Inlet to navigation because of the shoaling sands, which have made it impassable. The Little Egg Inlet remains open but is uncharted. It's well marked with buoys, but the Army Corps of Engineers must constantly re-mark the navigable channel. If you're running out of the inlet from Great Bay to the ocean, you won't find a straight channel to the offshore buoy. Unlike the Manasquan or Shark River Inlets, you'll instead find dogleg turns that weave their way around the treacherous shoals for about 2 miles. Any boater here who's unfamiliar with the bottom topography is risking running aground, particularly at low tide or when conditions are rough. This inlet is better left to the locals and the more experienced fishermen.

The locals who regularly fish these shoals, by the way, paint a different picture of this inlet. Many refer to it as one of the safest in New Jersey. Once you do know where the unmarked channels between the shoals are located, you can find four ways out to the ocean. These pathways allow you to duck behind a bar if the wind or waves are coming in an unfavorable direction.

The majority of the fishing opportunities here are by boat. All species of fish discussed in the text are available throughout the season with the exceptions of albacore and bonito. These two species don't make an appearance with any kind of consistency the way they do in the Barnegat Inlet 22 miles to the north.

The Little Egg Inlet is best known for its exceptional striper fishery from October through December. The peak usually occurs around the second or third week in October. The best way to hook into big bass is to drift live eels across the shoals. Short drifts working the ledges of the shoals are favored over long drifts through the channels. When the waves are throwing white water over the bars, you'll want to drift your boat along the edges and allow your eel to drop into the ledges and cutouts. Bass of up to 50 pounds can be taken, and fish in the 20- to 30-pound range are common.

If you choose to drift through the channels, you'll find that their depths fluctuate greatly. Depths will vary from 7 or 8 feet all the way up to a 90-foot stretch that extends for about 1/3 mile just inside the last buoy chain.

RIGGING LIVE EELS

The setup that most seasoned anglers use when drifting eels along drop-offs consists of a heavy-action rod in the 7- to 8-foot range and a conventional reel spooled with 20- to 30-pound test. Use a size 5/0 to 7/0 Gamakatsu octopus-style bait hook snelled to a 24- to 36-inch piece of 30- to 50-pound fluorocarbon. This leader length can vary depending on how fast the current is flowing and how finicky the bass are. In the daytime make sure to use a high-quality fluorocarbon leader. This will reduce its visibility in the water.

Tie your leader to a 100-pound barrel swivel and slide an egg sinker of from 1 to 4 ounces onto your main running line; the exact weight depends on conditions. Now tie your main running line to the other end of the barrel swivel. Hook your eel under the chin and through the eye socket, and you're ready to go.

Some anglers opt for a slightly different setup to get their eels to the bottom, tying in another barrel swivel behind the egg sinker. This section should be about 6 inches long and allow your egg sinker to slide on the line only along this distance. This will help ensure that your weight stays near the eel, keeping it on the bottom. A rubber-core sinker would achieve the same effect, but it also offers much more resistance when a bass picks up the eel.

A third method is to use a three-way swivel that attaches your leader to your main running line. To this add a 6- to 12-inch drop leader to which you tie your weight. Use a lighter pound test on the drop leader when bouncing the bottom this way: If you get hung up, it will easily break off, leaving your main leader with the eel intact.

Another location to check out with your boat is inside the Little Egg Inlet about 3 miles to the west between the marshes of Egg Island and Fish Island. This is Grassy Channel; it's found along the Intracoastal Waterway between markers 130 and 135.

This area is productive for stripers in early spring and weakfish into June. Small bluefish of up to 4 or 5 pounds can also be caught along the channel edges and up into the flats. Water depths at this location can range up to 12 feet.

Foot access to the inlet is extremely limited. Basically, you have two options. First, you can access the inlet from the southernmost end of Long Beach Island at Holgate. You can either walk the stretch (about 2 nautical miles) from the last beach access point to the tip or obtain a beach buggy permit and drive down. Beach buggy operations are closed from April through September, however, to protect migrating birds.

Your second option is to take Great Bay Boulevard in Tuckerton all the way to its end. You'll cross five bridges over some of the bay's small channels. The last two bridges are one-lane wooden structures that completely immerse you in the ambience of the surrounding environment. At certain high tides this roadway can be flooded and inaccessible, so coordinating your fishing with the timing of the tides is important.

Once you reach the end of the road, just follow the path that leads to the inlet. You'll see the old Coast Guard station to your right. This building now houses the Center for Environmental Studies of the Marine Science Center of Rutgers University. The area in front, known as the Shooting Thoroughfare, is an excellent place to fish. It's best known as an ideal place for fly fishers to hook into nice-quality bass along the sod banks.

The Shooting Thoroughfare channel drops off from wading depth to 25 feet or so within casting distance of a long rod. The prime time to hit this location is from the second week in June through the second week of July. Using patterns such as white Snake Flies or large Deceivers on sinking lines is an effective way to fish this current.

To get to the Little Egg Inlet via land, take Route 539 to Route 9 and turn right. Go straight to the fork in the road and bear left. This is Great Bay Boulevard (Seven Bridges Road). Follow this road to its end, and you're there.

GRAVELING POINT, TUCKERTON
RADIO ROAD/CREEK MOUTH/POINT

As January and February usher in their cold northwest winds, Jersey anglers flock to boat shows and fishing seminars trying to find a cure for cabin fever. Not being able to cast a line into the suds for two months is enough to drive an avid angler crazy. But as March rolls around the prolonged wait is finally over, and the return of warmer temperatures gets the fish on the move again. At this time of year just one phone call or e-mail announcing fish being caught is all it takes to send us scurrying for the rods. Without even thinking twice anglers will travel from one end of the state to the other to wet a line.

One of the first places in New Jersey where consistent and legitimate action takes place is at Graveling Point in Little Egg Harbor Township. Graveling Point is located in the Mystic Island section of this township and is part of the Edwin B. Forsythe National Wildlife Refuge.

This point starts to produce bass by the second week in March, and fish remain in good numbers until the first week in May. Since the point is situated at the mouth of the Mullica River, which empties into Great Bay, a warm-water influx feeds this location and acts like a magnet drawing in stripers.

The tip of the point is the place to get set up and can easily accommodate 10 fishermen. As the point gets crowded, anglers spread out along the banks; on a nice spring day you'll easily find 50 anglers or more here. Two to three hundred fishermen will visit this location on a weekend day when the word is out that the fish are here. Parking is limited along Radio Road, the access that leads out to the point. Much of the area is posted because of the townhouse developments along the banks of Great Bay. You'll need to plan accordingly and get here early if it's a nice day.

In the early part of spring, particularly March and April, the outgoing tide produces the best results. At low tide you'll find water in the 3- to 8-foot range directly out in front; at high tide this increases to 6 to 11 feet. It isn't until the early part of May that the better activity will be on the incoming tide as cooler waters from the ocean are brought in.

The preferred method of hooking into stripers is dead sticking with bloodworms. Most locals use high-low or pompano rigs with 3/0 bronze baitholder hooks. The bait should sit on or float just above the bottom, because the fish are lethargic and want to see the baits. Thus the proper amount of weight is going to be vital to your success. At high tide when there's a strong rip, 6 to 8 ounces of lead will be needed to hold the bottom. Generally, however, 4 ounces will do.

Scott Albertson, a resident expert and the owner of Scott's Bait and Tackle, recommends that when you fish the point "you cast for all you're worth." You need to hit the 7- to 8-foot depths to really hook into the fish with any kind of consistency. This is about 200 feet out in front of you from the shoreline. Some really big spring stripers can be taken from this location in the early part of the season. Each spring Scott weighs 15 to 20 fish that tip the scales at better than 20 pounds. The local class of fish are barely keepers, however—30 inches and down.

As the first week in May arrives, the stripers begin to relocate and bluefish tend to dominate the area. Blues range in size from 1 1/2-pounders to the occasional fish in the 8- to 12-pound class. During this time the cooler incoming waters of the ocean will turn the fish on. Fly rodders can cash in on some great light-tackle action now, because there's plenty of room to backcast: The early-season crowds are gone, and most fishermen have taken to their boats. Even Scott comments that at this time of the season his sale of bloodworms drops from 35 boxes a week to 3. If you're heading out to the point, be sure to stop in to Scott's shop for the latest information and some friendly advice.

To get to Graveling Point, take Great Bay Boulevard in Tuckerton to Radio Road and make a right. Follow Radio Road to the end and park where you're sure you won't be ticketed. Walk out to the bay to Mystic Beach and make a right. As you walk along the beach, you'll come to a small creek that you'll have to cross to get to the point. Cross near its mouth, where a sandbar is located. The water toward the inside of the creek is too deep to cross, particularly during the high-tide stages of a new or full moon.

MULLICA RIVER

NACOTE CREEK, BASS RIVER, AND WADING
RIVER/DEEP POINT, AKIMBO POINT, BLOOD POINT,
MOSS POINT, AND COLLINS POINT/
CHESTNUT NECK BOAT YARD

If you're making an early-season run to Graveling Point to cash
in on the hot striper action, check out the Mullica River if you
have time. Located in the central Pinelands of southern New
Jersey, the Mullica borders Atlantic and Ocean Counties. Its 13-
mile tidal portion weaves its way through a maze of estuarine
wetlands and tidal marshes that are some of the most pristine
and diverse in all New Jersey.

The Mullica River is part of the largest watershed in the
Pinelands and is protected by either state or federal regulations.
Parts are included in the Edwin B. Forsythe National Wildlife
Refuge, the Great Bay Boulevard Wildlife Management Area, the
Port Republic Wildlife Management Area, the Swan Bay Wildlife
Management Area, and the Pinelands Management Area, along
with Wharton, Batsto, and Bass River State Forests. It was origi-
nally known as the Little Egg Harbor River and was renamed in
honor of Eric Mullica, a Swedish immigrant who established a
community along its banks in the 17th century.

The Mullica is one of the few unaltered rivers in our state
and supports a wide diversity of marine organisms, nesting birds,
plants, and animals. More than 90 different species of fish thrive
here. All the species mentioned in this text—with the exception
of the false albacore—can be caught in these waters.

The Mullica is another early-season hot spot for striped
bass. The fishery takes off during the second week of March, the
same time that you'll find action at its mouth at Graveling Point.
Fish become active as the water slowly warms due to increasing
sunlight and runoff from the surrounding creeks and tributaries.
The Mullica River supports an excellent population of holdover
bass and also supports spawning fish to some degree.

The mouth of the Mullica where it empties into Great Bay is an excellent place to try your luck in the early part of the season. Look for the deeper holes just off the banks. At its widest the mouth is approximately 1 1/2 miles across. As you move upriver, this distance narrows considerably. The fishing remains excellent all the way up to Swan Bay. The mouths of any of the tributaries, creeks, or rivers that empty into the Mullica along this route are worth investigating. The Nacote Creek, Bass River, and Wading River should not be overlooked.

As you move upriver you'll also come across many points with nice drop-offs and good currents refracting around their edges. Deep Point, Akimbo Point, Blood Point, Moss Point, and Collins Point are just a few to check out.

There are strong currents and tidal flows through the Mullica, and the water is much deeper than in many of our other tidal rivers. In the main channel depths range from 8 to 30 feet. The drop-offs and ledges along the banks are always productive in early spring.

One spot frequently visited by early-season anglers is located just off the Garden State Parkway at the Chestnut Neck Boat Yard. The area around the marina and up along the banks to the Parkway Bridge is very productive for early-season stripers. Easy access to the water makes this location very popular.

At this time of year the preferred method for taking stripers is dead sticking with bloodworms. A high-low rig tied to 8- to 12-pound test is all you need, because the majority of the stripers you catch will be small. Given the colder water temperatures, you'll find days when the fish can be rather lethargic, rarely moving much to take a bait. When the bite is slow in one area try moving to another hole or drop-off to see if there are fish lying below.

At other times the stripers will become active on the changing tide, milling around and nosing through the bottom to pick up baits. The best action is usually found on the top of the high tide as it begins to drop. Patience is important at this time of year; the do-nothing approach is most productive. Drop your baits in the water and leave them there. This can be difficult, of course—particularly if the weather is on the raw side.

As the water warms into late April and early May, the bass become more active and begin to hit a variety of swimming plugs. These plugs can be cast from the banks or your boat, or trolled at a slow swimming speed. Small Bombers, Rapalas, Red Fins, and Megabaits all account for fish. The key is to cast up toward the bank and retrieve the plug over the ledges or drop-offs.

If you're trolling a plug on a flat line from the back of your boat, the plug's action is critical to your success. Make sure it's wobbling or slowly moving from side to side. To achieve the desired plug action you'll need to pay attention to the direction that the current is flowing, the direction and speed that you're traveling, and whether the wind is with you or against you. Also keep in mind that each plug runs differently under these varying conditions. Eliminate as much terminal tackle on the plug as you can by simply tying a small snap directly to your leader. To keep your line from getting twisted, place a small barrel swivel about 4 to 5 feet up from the end of the snap. You can also opt for a small good-quality barrel swivel clipped directly to the plug.

Later in the month a good population of herring moves into the river to spawn, and you can take some rather large stripers by live-lining these baits. Boats equipped with a large live well will be able to keep a small number of herring alive during the course of the day. These baits are very fragile and require a lot of oxygen to stay alive. Try to avoid having a large amount of foam on top of the water; you can buy foam inhibitants over the counter to keep this at a minimum.

Care should also be taken when transporting the baits from their pen to the live well or when taking the baits from the live well to place on your hook. Use a soft net with small holes so the herring don't get their gills or fins tangled. This would just cause undue stress to the baits as you try to free them. Once hooked behind the dorsal, get them in the water as soon as possible.

The Mullica is also known for supporting a good weak-fish population as June rolls around. Drifting sandworms in any of the deeper holes or near the mouth of the river will definitely get you your limit. You can also try live-lining a small snapper blue or spot for some larger fish.

You can access the Mullica River from the Chestnut Neck Boat Yard on Route 9 East, just off exit 48 from the Garden Sate Parkway. Or leave the parkway at exit 58 and head east on Route 539. Make a right onto Route 9 and then a left onto Great Bay Boulevard. Travel 1/4 mile to Radio Road and make a right. At the end of the road you'll see Great Bay Marina on your left.

When live lining a bait, handle them carefully. Place the hook just below the dorsal and above the spine. Jim Freda

BRIGANTINE

LITTLE BEACH/BRIGANTINE SHOALS/BRIGANTINE INLET/BRIGANTINE CHANNEL/SUNKEN CLAM BOAT/OLD COAST GUARD STATION/ABSECON INLET/ROUTE 87 BRIDGE/RUM POINT

South of the Little Egg Inlet are the third and fourth barrier islands that protect our state's coastline. The first island, Pullen Island or Little Beach, is 2 1/2 miles long and better known as the Edwin B. Forsythe National Wildlife Refuge, one of the largest pristine wetlands in the Northeast. This beach is off limits to fishing and offers no wadable access. The U.S. Fish and Wildlife Service oversees it. You can fish the front beach by boat, but exercise caution: The shallow bar just off the beach produces hazardous breakers.

Directly across from Pullen Island is Brigantine (the two islands are separated by the Brigantine Inlet), the only city island in New Jersey. This 6-mile-long island was once home to such legendary pirates as Captain Kidd and Blackbeard, and it's alleged that they buried treasure along its beaches. The island's name is derived from the 17th-century sailing ships that were habitually wrecked off the Brigantine Shoals just to the east. These shoals are some of the most feared and respected in the state, and stretch for more than a mile parallel to the beach.

At the northernmost end of the island is the Brigantine Inlet. This is an unimproved inlet with no jetties and is extremely dangerous to use as an outlet to the ocean. An extensive sandbar lies directly down its center, and treacherous breakers await you off its mouth. Only on extremely calm days will a handful of locals cut over these shoals at high tide on their way out to the ocean. Boaters seeking access to the ocean should use the Absecon Inlet to the south. To the locals the Brigantine Inlet has long been known as Wreck Inlet.

Between the Brigantine Shoals and the mouth of the inlet you'll find good bottom structure—humps and ledges. Some of the local sharpies who are extremely familiar with this area work it for stripers by jigging bucktails or drifting live eels along the bottom.

The waters on the inside of the inlet are known as Brigantine Channel. Locals access this channel through Bonita Tideway and Obes Thoroughfare. Most anglers troll diving plugs along the sod banks and catch good numbers of stripers and weakfish throughout the season. The creek mouths of Mud Thoroughfare and Weakfish Thoroughfare that empty into Brigantine Channel have quick drop-offs and are worth investigating.

If you want to fish the inlet area on foot, you'll need a vehicle and a buggy permit. The last beach entrance is approximately 2 1/2 miles to the south. This area at the mouth of the inlet and on its inside does offer excellent fishing from shore: You can walk all along the sod banks well back into the channel. This is a great place for fly fishers to cast, since there are no waves or white water, and there's nothing to impede your backcast. On days when the wind is blowing off the ocean, this is the place to be.

As you move south of the inlet, you'll find two areas along the beach that locals regularly fish; both are worth investigating. I was fortunate enough to have as my guide to this area lifelong resident and fisherman Bill Ferris, who gave me the grand tour. Bill pointed out the sunken clam boat and the old Coast Guard station pilings that remain on the beach as two spots with good holes directly in front of them. He recommends fishing these locations whenever you are traveling along the northern part of the island. Bill adds that the best striper fishing in Brigantine is from the middle of October to the end of December. A favorite artificial for the locals is a yellow or white bucktail tipped with squid. The trick is to marinate the squid in sheddar oil for several days before you use it.

You'll see much wider beaches at the southern end of Brigantine Island due to a north–south littoral current. At the seawall located at 14th Street North and East Brigantine Avenue the water comes right up to walkway. Recent replenishment projects have kept this area from eroding away to the point that large storms will cause damage to the beachfront infrastructure; more such projects are planned.

At the southernmost end of Brigantine is the Absecon Inlet, which separates the island from Atlantic City directly to the south. This is the widest improved inlet in New Jersey. From the Brigantine side of the inlet you can gain access to the jetty with a beach buggy permit by driving directly to it. On foot, walk south along the beach or access the base of the jetty back by the cove at Pepper Cove Lane at the end of Ocean Drive South. This is by far the best of the few jetties on the island.

As you move northwest into the inlet, you'll find that excellent fishing is available either by boat or on foot. A deep channel along the Brigantine side of the inlet drops off to 30 feet. The area directly in front of Rum Point has current and a well-differentiated bottom; lumps, ledges, and shell beds are all present. Drifting eels or bouncing bucktails along this point is a favorite way to hook into big bass and weakfish.

Farther up the inlet you'll come to the Route 87 Bridge that connects Brigantine to Atlantic City. Working the deeper water under this bridge is very effective, particularly around the abutments. This entire area is also accessible on foot from the Brigantine side of the bridge. Veteran fisherman Ron Wertz showed me the ropes here, pointing out that as soon as you cross over the bridge you'll find a dirt turnoff on the left side of the road that takes you down to the water below the bridge. Here the remains of the old bridge have been left intact and extend out over the water. You can fish from here or walk along the sod banks either east or west.

These sod banks are a favorite location for weakfish in May and June. Ron says that nighttime fishing here is extremely productive. Weakies in the 9- to 10-pound class are caught each spring by anglers throwing Fin-S Fish or flies. You can walk the sod banks up to Rum Point and wade out onto the bar to get close to the edge of the channel. When walking these sod banks—or any sod banks in New Jersey, for that matter—be very careful, because many are soft, are undercut, and drop off quickly. Very swift currents usually run along their edges.

Beach buggy access in Brigantine is available year-round, except for the north section past the old Coast Guard station; this is closed for piping plover nesting from approximately May 15 through August 15. A permit costs $100 and can be obtained from city hall or Lifeguard Headquarters at 17th Street and the beach. Beach access points are located at the north end entrance at 15th Street and the jetty entrance at Seaside. The cove entrance at the end of Lagoon Boulevard is open from 7 A.M. to 7 P.M.

You can reach Brigantine Island at its southern end. Take the Garden State Parkway south to exit 40. This will put you on Route 30, White Horse Pike East. Follow the signs to Brigantine, taking Route 87 North over the bridge by Harrah marina.

OCEAN DRIVE

The 40 miles of New Jersey coast that stretch from Atlantic City to Cape May Point are inundated with islands, wetlands, channels, bays, and sounds. Many of the areas are pristine and offer some of the most scenic views that New Jersey has to offer. Before 1940 traveling along the coast to see these sights was difficult—wherever you turned there was water in the way. Today this is no longer the case. In 1938 an act of the New Jersey Legislature created the Cape May County Bridge Commission. The bridges that this commission constructed now allow you to travel along Ocean Drive for the entire distance. This concrete and steel network weaves its way along the beaches, through the wetlands, and across the inlets and sounds, providing access to the many beaches, recreational areas, and prime fishing locations that are available in southern New Jersey. At its southernmost end you can jump aboard the Cape May–Lewes Ferry and boat across Delaware Bay to Lewes, Delaware.

ATLANTIC CITY

T-JETTY, ABSECON INLET/HACKNEYS PIER
/BEACH/PUBLIC DOCK, HARRAH'S MARINA

The Jersey shore's fifth barrier island protecting the mainland is Absecon Island, home to one of the nation's most popular destinations—Atlantic City. Absecon Island is approximately 10 miles long and is bordered to the north by the Absecon Inlet, to the south by the Great Egg Harbor Inlet. West of the island are the creeks and channels of Absecon, Lakes, and Scull Bays.

Atlantic City, originally known as Absecon Beach, begins at the northernmost end of the island and stretches approximately 6 miles southward. The remaining towns of Ventnor, Margate City, and Longport round out the southernmost end of the island.

Atlantic City takes center stage here with its glamour and glitter and world-class entertainment. It's best known for its 12 gambling casinos, the world's first boardwalk, and the Miss America Pageant, while the southern end of the island offers the ambience of a quaint, upscale seaside community.

The first visitors to Atlantic City were the Assegai Indians of the Lenni Lenape tribe. They traveled from the mainland to the island across the Old Indian Trail, located where Florida Avenue is found today. The Indians reaped a bountiful harvest from the unsettled island.

The city was incorporated in 1854, and grand-sounding street names were put in place. Those running parallel to the ocean were named for the world's great bodies of water: Pacific, Atlantic, Baltic, Mediterranean, Adriatic, and Arctic. The streets running east to west were named for the states.

A contingent of local surf anglers regularly works the beaches and back bay waters here to hook into any of the species mentioned in this text, but for the most part the area is not known for attracting fishermen. The biggest obstacles are traffic congestion from tourists and limited parking. This is not to say that the area isn't home to some excellent fishing. In fact, some very large fish roam these waters—including the current IGFA all-tackle world-record striped bass, which was caught off the Vermont Avenue Jetty by Al McReynolds on September 21, 1982.

This fish tipped the scales at 78 pounds, 8 ounces, and was 53 inches long. The bass had a girth of 53 inches and was determined by state biologists to be a female born in 1946. Al caught the fish on a 5 1/2-inch black-backed Rebel minnow fished on 20-pound Ande line. This monster took an hour and 40 minutes to land. Many skilled surf fishermen have since earnestly worked these waters in the hope of similar good fortune.

There are several locations that are worth investigating if you're in the area. The first is the T-Jetty at the mouth of the Absecon Inlet. This jetty can be accessed from Oriental Avenue at the northernmost end of Absecon Island and is a good location to catch stripers, bluefish, and weakfish.

The jetty is approximately 200 feet long and offers more protection from the havoc that Mother Nature can wreak than do the jetties along the beachfront. The island curves toward the mainland at this northern end, avoiding a direct hit from the crashing surf. This jetty is very easy to walk on due to its flat-topped cement-filled construction. As a result, you'll usually find plenty of fishermen here throughout the season.

The construction of this jetty was intended to stop severe erosion that was threatening the Absecon Lighthouse along the

Atlantic City has much to offer in the way of fishing, despite the crowds that are drawn by its lavish casinos. Jim Freda photo.

water's edge. Today this historic lighthouse can be found sitting several blocks from the ocean in a residential area due to the shoaling of sand. A drive down Pacific Avenue will bring you to the lighthouse, which was first lit in 1857 and dramatically reduced the number of shipwrecks that occurred outside the Absecon Inlet, known at the time as the "Graveyard Inlet."

At the base of the T-Jetty is the northernmost portion of the Atlantic City boardwalk, which sits about 15 feet above the surface of the water. It's a good spot to fish and relax. The inlet water runs for a short distance under the boardwalk, which provides an excellent casting platform. To get to the T-Jetty, head down Atlantic Avenue until you get to New Hampshire Avenue, make a right, and then turn left onto Oriental Avenue. Parking is very limited along these side streets; many require a residential permit for extended hours.

A second location frequented daily by fishermen is the seawall at the end of New Hampshire Avenue across from the Coast Guard station. This seawall, also known as Hackneys Pier, is a black steel bulkhead that provides easy access and relaxing fishing for anglers of all ages. There's a large parking area here; you can pull right up to the wall and begin fishing. Many local old-timers fish this area and can offer you a wealth of information, plus some plain old good conversation.

All species of fish can be caught along the wall during the appropriate season, along with some sea bass and porgies. Either spin or conventional methods will work, but most anglers prefer to bait up and just sit back and relax. Just behind this area you will find the historic Gardner's Basin where pirates and Revolutionary privateers took shelter. Look for the Fisherman's Museum and new Ocean Life Center Aquarium here, too.

Also worth investigating are the jetties that stretch along the beachfront. Many anglers have come here with the hope of hooking into another world record. And who knows? It could happen here, or just about anywhere along the coast. A final location that draws anglers is the public dock at Harrah's Marina. This dock is well fenced, lit at night, and about 100 feet long. Good currents travel around the dock on a moving tide. Stripers and weakfish can be caught from here, particularly at night when the boat traffic is down. Drifting live eels around the dock is very effective for some bigger fish.

LANDING A TROPHY FISH

Trophy hunting is a passion for many New Jersey anglers. Landing that 40- or 50-pounder is definitely the ultimate in fishing excitement. If you're trophy hunting along the beach, here's a short list of considerations that you should pay attention to:

• Fighting a trophy fish will require all your wits, skills, and a little bit of luck. Put the odds in your favor by being prepared with the right equipment. Use conventional, spin, or fly tackle rated for heavy action. This will give you the power and leverage, the line capacity, and the line retrieval ratio per crank to best subdue your catch.

• Use a high-quality leader material in the 25- to 40-pound-test range. Don't count the pennies in this department. Many of us spend a small fortune on our rods and reels; it's silly to try to economize on leaders. Remember, this is your most important connection to the fish.

• Sharpen all your hooks before you make your first cast. Use good-quality stainless-steel hooks. This will give you the needed penetration when you set the hook into the bony palate of a bass. Large bass will strike out and hit your artificial very aggressively, but don't be fooled into thinking the hook is properly set. Lay back on your rod with considerable force while putting a hefty bend in the rod.

• After hooking up, try to remain calm; don't panic even though your adrenaline is surging. Don't try to turn the fish's head while it's running. Just hold on and let your rod and reel drag do the work. Enjoy the run. Don't make any adjustments in your drag, either. If it was set properly from the start, tightening down now will result in a breakoff. Once the run is over you can regain line by pumping and reeling down on the fish in short segments.

- *Never point your rod tip directly at the fish during any part of your battle. Maintain a hefty bend in the rod while keeping it off to the side at a slight angle above the water. This will reduce the amount of pressure on the leader. Don't fight your fish with the rod held vertically.*
- *Keep constant pressure on your bass. Letting up will give the fish time to recuperate and regain energy. It will also cause slack in the line that may allow the hook to fall out. Remember, the penetration hole gets larger as the fight ensues.*
- *If you're on a jetty, pay attention to the direction that your trophy is running. If the fish runs to the right, turn and lower your rod to the left. If the fish runs to the left, turn and lower your rod to the right. Applying side pressure in this manner will keep the most pressure on the fish.*
- *If you're on a jetty and unable to walk the fish off the rocks, make sure you have a predetermined landing route in mind. Look for flat rocks near the water's edge—but always keep one eye on the approaching waves.*
- *Once your fish is in the zone of the breakers, look for a wave to help push it toward the beach. Reel quickly, taking up any slack that occurs, and reset the hook when the line draws tight. Be cognizant of an energetic backwash that will forcefully draw your fish back into the surf as it approaches the sand. Use your reeling hand to quickly feed line from your reel to the fish if this happens.*
- *Finally, fish your artificials with confidence. Believe that a trophy will hit each time you cast. If you put in your time on the water, one eventually will.*

To get to Harrah's Dock, take the Garden State Parkway south to exit 40 to White Horse Pike East (Route 30). Follow the signs to Brigantine. Exit at Dr. Martin Luther King Boulevard (Illinois Avenue) and turn left. Follow the signs to Harrah's.

OCEAN CITY

GREAT EGG HARBOR INLET/
LONGPORT JETTY/RAINBOW CHANNEL

The sixth barrier island along our coast is the 9-mile stretch of sand known as Ocean City. It's bordered to the north by the Great Egg Harbor Inlet and to the south by Corson Inlet State Park. This entire area is well known as a great family vacation spot with a boardwalk, rides, great restaurants, and other attractions.

For my visit to Ocean City I had the pleasure of meeting with Captain Bryan DiLeo of Iowa Fortune Guide Service. Captain Bryan is a full-time professional guide and well respected in the area as a first-rate captain. He provided me with the bulk of my information on this area. He also introduced me to a whole new world of striper fishing that most people associate with the Florida Keys, not New Jersey.

Captain Bryan's specialty is sight fishing for bass on the extensive flats behind Atlantic City and Ocean City. He was one of the first captains to introduce a flats boats to these waters. Imagine poling through skinny water of no more than 12 inches shooting a fly to teen-sized bass right here in your own backyard! And being able to see your quarry adds the extra rush of adrenaline that makes this type of fishing so exciting. Captain Bryan sums it up nicely by saying that when these fish hit a fly, "They will take off like a rocket, with nowhere to go but out. You can expect fish to peel off in excess of 50 yards of line on their first run."

The northern end of the island is most productive. According to Captain Bryan, this is due to the strong ocean influences it receives from the Great Egg Harbor Inlet. The Corson Inlet, at the southern end of the island, is much smaller and has more of an estuarine nature due to the lesser volume of water that moves through it.

You'll find the bulk of Ocean City's fishable jetties from 10th Street north. These jetties are flat topped, but they're not filled with concrete (as we see in the more central and northern parts of our state). South of 10th Street there are some small finger jetties, but these are usually submerged at high tide. The typical beach profile is a gradual slope with a shifting sandbar approximately 100 yards off. Beyond the bar the ocean bottom tapers gradually; depths of only about 30 feet are found 3 miles out. The north–south littoral current is evident by the wider beaches to the north and narrow beaches at the island's southern end.

Along the oceanfront beach buggy access is permitted from September 15 to May 15. The permit fee is $75 and is limited to 300; a waiting list is in effect. Permits can be obtained from the police station. Beach access points are located at 23rd Street, 57th Street, and 59th Street.

Stripers, weakfish, and bluefish are the mainstay of the fishery in Ocean City. Summer and winter flounder can be caught in the backwaters of Rainbow Channel, Great Egg Harbor Bay, Peck Bay, and Corson Sound, but these fish seem to be less popular than they are farther north.

If your target is big stripers and weakfish, you'll want to fish the Great Egg Harbor Inlet. This inlet is approximately 1 1/4 miles across and can be fished by boat or from the beach. In a boat, be careful to remain in the marked channel. There are no long jetties to protect this inlet from the mighty Atlantic. On both sides of the inlet you'll find shoals and bars that extend for about a mile directly off each tip. These areas have frequent breakers, and trying to navigate through cuts in the shoals can be extremely hazardous. You should run out toward the GE Bell before you attempt to turn north or south along the beach.

As you drift through the inlet's main channel you'll find some solid depths in the 30- to 40-foot range. The striper fishing is excellent here, particularly in spring and fall. A favorite method to hook into these burly linesiders is to jig with bucktails using 7-inch Culprit Curly Tail Worms as trailers. Captain Bryan recommends using the pearl blue and firetail colors. Don't be surprised if you hook into some nice-sized weakfish, too.

You can also spin fish or fly fish either side of the inlet on foot. On the north side of the inlet is the town of Longport, where a small jetty provides a direct link to the inlet's channel. This jetty can comfortably hold about 12 fishermen. More than this and it's crowded. This jetty coves around to the ocean side, where another small jetty is located. You can walk around from one to the other on the rocks; there's a small seawall between the two. In this cove you'll find good bass action on a northeast blow. You'll also find good concentrations of mullet and peanut bunker getting trapped here in fall.

The northern point of Ocean City provides good access to the inlet via its south side. The beach is wide open with no rock jetties until you make your way around the point to the ocean side. The distance you can cover is approximately 3 miles.

At this location you can also wade out to the northern bar off the point and fish the rips formed as the water exchanges on the tides. You can reach this bar only during a spring low tide (new- or full-moon tide). It's best to wade out to the bar toward the end of the outgoing tide. On an incoming tide you'll have to be careful, because the area will backfill behind you. There's a small parking area on the Ocean City side of the toll bridge that leads over to Longport; you can park here and walk out to the point. Currently a new bridge is under construction. Part of the old bridge will be left as a fishing pier.

Some of the best fishing you'll encounter in the northern section of Ocean City is behind the barrier island, in the bay, channels, and thoroughfares. According to Captain Bryan, the fishing can really heat up in these backwaters due to the strong tidal flows that will push or pull water through. Rainbow Channel and Thoroughfare, Great Egg Harbor Bay, and Peck Bay are all hot spots for bass and weakfish throughout the entire season. Night fishing for bass is also very productive, because the extensive array of islands draws bait and forage into the shallows.

During the daylight hours you'll see Captain Bryan poling his way around sight fishing for bass in these parts. October is the best month for finding the biggest bass on the flats. Bryan recommends using tackle as light as you can get away with in this skinny water. A fly rod is even better. Bryan uses a combination of traditional flies such as Clousers and Deceivers but also employs a good mix of nontraditionals like Tarpon Bunnies, crab patterns, Crease Flies, and gurglers to take bass. The key to fool

A flats boat is a very effective way for working the skinny back bay waters for stripers. Captain Bryan DiLeo shows how it's done.
Elizabeth DiLeo photo.

ing these fish, however, is approaching them in silence. A low-profile stalking technique is critical.

You can locate Rainbow Channel as you head out to Ocean City from Somers Point. There are four bridges you'll need to cross. The first and second bridges go over Elbow Thoroughfare, while the third goes over Rainbow Channel. The fourth and last bridge is the drawbridge. You can access Rainbow Channel on foot by parking on the north side of the bridge. If you're in your boat, be aware that this bridge is not passable. If you're drifting the north side you'll have to go back to Elbow Thoroughfare and make your way around the Rainbow Islands to get to the south side of the channel.

To get to the northern end of Ocean City, take exit 30 off the Garden State Parkway. You'll be in the town of Somers Point. Follow Route 52 East for about a mile; the signs then change to Route 52 South. Follow this for approximately 3 1/2 miles directly into Ocean City.

To access the Longport Jetty from Ocean City go over the toll bridge into the town of Longport. At the end of Atlantic Avenue you'll find a small parking lot that can hold eight cars. The jetty will be directly in front of you. You can also head south from Atlantic City through Margate, Ventnor, and into Longport.

CORSON INLET STATE PARK

LAUNCH RAMP/RUSH CHATTIN BRIDGE/ INTRACOASTAL WATERWAY/POINT

Of the 12 New Jersey inlets I've fished, the Corson Inlet stands out in my mind as unique. It's an unimproved inlet with no rock jetties, but there's plenty of access for the boat, spin, and fly fisherman. It's located between Ocean City and Strathmere. Estuarine features coupled with a covelike nature create a setting where you can find a tranquil environment away from the pounding surf.

Corson Inlet State Park was established in 1969 to protect and preserve one of the few remaining tracts of undeveloped land along the oceanfront. It's a series of sandy primary and secondary dunes with lush vegetation and diversified wildlife. Part of the New Jersey Coastal Heritage Trail, it offers hiking, boating, fishing, and a mobile sport-fishing program.

One of the unique features of Corson is the public boat launch, which gives you access to the back bay waters, the Corson Inlet, and the ocean on a very calm day. The ramp is located adjacent to the Rush Chattin Bridge on Ocean Drive. It's a concrete ramp that's well maintained but narrow. There's no bulkhead or floating dock, and for this reason only one boat should be launched at a time, for safety. This ramp is very popular and can get crowded, particularly in summertime. You should be prepared for a waiting line on nice days. Also note that the beach on either side of it has many submerged rocks; when returning to the ramp, be careful not to run your boat onto it.

Once you're in the water there are plenty of back waterways to fish. You can anchor up under the Rush Chattin Bridge and fish the deeper waters of the channel and around the bridge pilings. This is an excellent location for bigger stripers and weakfish. Or you can try the extensive flats that weave their way back through the thoroughfares. The Intracoastal Waterway, Corson Sound, and Ludlam Bay are all accessible.

If you head out toward the ocean, you should be aware that the inlet itself is very difficult to navigate. It isn't very wide, and there are shoaling bars and breakers across its entrance. The Great Egg Harbor Inlet is the way to go if you're looking to head out into the ocean. You can, however, drift back through the inlet on an incoming tide. In summer and fall drifting sandworms or bouncing jigs along the bottom at night is a very effective way to hook some nice stripers or weakfish.

The Corson Inlet also provides plenty of access for the surf caster or fly fisherman. From the parking lot by the launch ramp you can walk to your left along the dune-protected beach all the way to the inlet. This distance is close to a mile. Here you can cast bait or plugs or shoot flies into the calm waters of the estuary. This area behind the dunes is a favorite for fly fishers. You can wade out into the water and work the drop-offs and ledges. A good cast will put you into 10 to 14 feet of water. Intermediate fly lines are usually the lines of choice, but if the current is moving you'll want to switch to a 250- or 300-grain line.

If you walk to the end of the beach you'll come to the point. This is one of the most popular locations, because a nice rip is formed here on the changing tides. You can work your way around the point toward the ocean, casting as you go. You'll

Corson Inlet State Park offers a free public boat launch and good fishing access from the Rush Chattin Bridge. Jim Freda photo.

often see busting fish as they set up on the bait being swept through this area.

You can also access the Corson Inlet from its Strathmere side. To do this, go over the toll bridge into Strathmere and make a quick left onto Willard Avenue. Follow this to the corner of Seaview and Commonwealth Avenues, and you'll see the Strathmere Natural Area that is part of Corson Inlet Sate Park. There's a path you can follow to the water.

The Corson Inlet also offers beach buggy access from September 15 to May 15. A permit costs $25 and can be obtained from Corson Inlet State Park, P.O. Box 450, Woodbine, NJ 08270. The beach access point is a marked gate at the end of Central Avenue.

Adjacent to the launch ramp is the Rush Chattin Bridge, which spans the back of the inlet's waters that lead to the Intracoastal Waterway. Crossing the bridge will bring you to the toll bridge that leads into Strathmere. This bridge was designed with fishermen and kids in mind. Fishing access is provided on its northwest side. The steel bridge has a fishing platform that spans its length. It's well railed and safe for the kids to drop a line. Not only can you experience some very good fishing here, but you can also enjoy the picturesque view of the inlet. This is a great aerial shot and a place where you don't want to be without your camera. Parking can be found as you go over the bridge toward Strathmere; look for a small parking area directly to your right. A Porta-Potti is also available at this location.

If you fish the center of the bridge, you'll find that the current runs swiftly between its concrete pilings. You'll need a heavy weight to hold on or near the bottom. The main channel is about 35 feet deep. For this reason either slack high or slack low tide will put you closest to the bottom. As you move toward the ends of the bridge, the water will be shallower and the current not as swift. You can catch stripers, blues, weakfish, and both flounder in this area.

BRIDGE FISHING

If you're serious about your bridge fishing, you'll need some type of bridge gaff or net to lift a big fish. Remember, if the fish isn't legal length, you can't gaff it. Instead, you can walk it off the bridge (which may or may not be possible); you can try to lift it (which may result in your line breaking); or—the preferred method—you can net the fish using a specially designed bridge net. Most bridge nets are constructed of a hoop of PVC with netting. Drop yours next to the fish by attaching a clip to your main running line and allowing the net to fall into the water. Ropes are attached so you can raise the net along with your catch.

Most veteran bridge fishermen use a three-point bridge gaff for legal fish that are headed for the dinner table. Place the bridge gaff onto your line through a slit in the gaff's weighted head section. Then slide it down to the head of the fish by means of a rope. The three large wide-gap hooks are set on pins so that they'll spread open around the head of the fish when the gaff comes in contact with it. The hooks will hold the fish, and then you can lift everything by means of the attached rope. These bridge gaffs are strong and are capable of lifting a 30- or 40- pound fish if you can muster up enough muscle.

To get to Corson Inlet State Park, travel south on Ocean Drive through Ocean City. Just before you get to the Rush Chattin Bridge you'll see the entrance to the parking lot on your left. This is also where the public boat launch is located.

Sea Isle City

STRATHMERE/SEA ISLE 1ST–93RD STREETS/ TOWNSENDS INLET/LUDLAM BAY/FLAT CREEK

New Jersey's seventh barrier island is a 6 1/2-mile stretch of sand bordered on the north by the Corson Inlet, and by the Townsends Inlet to the south. Here you'll find the municipalities of Strathmere, Sea Isle City, and Townsends Inlet.

When researching this area I had the pleasure of speaking with Captain Joe Hughes, of Jersey Cape Guide Service. He's well known on the island and is also the manager of Gibson's Bait and Tackle in Sea Isle City.

Beginning at the northernmost end of the island, Captain Joe recommends fishing the point at Strathmere that's at the mouth of the Corson Inlet. Here sandbars and shoals extending out into the ocean are productive. The shallow nature of this area produces a lot of white water that attracts some nice-sized bass, particularly in fall.

On the bay side of the point behind Strathmere you'll find a number of good holes that at times can extend down to 40 feet. Captain Joe points out that these holes are constantly changing in depth due to the strong tidal influences of the inlet. This area is known as an excellent weakfish location in spring; large tiderunners are caught on a regular basis.

As you move around to the ocean side, you'll notice a north to south littoral current that runs along the entire island. As a result, the beaches to the south are wider. In Strathmere look for four sets of wooden pilings along the beach; these have good holes along their sides. Fishing along these pilings is usually productive, particularly during high tides.

From 1st to 30th Street in Sea Isle City you'll find all open beach. You can drive on the beach here with a beach buggy permit; you'll also find buggy access from 56th to 93rd Street. There's no beach buggy access in downtown Sea Isle City proper. Captain Joe says that since the open beach is very shallow, you really need the presence of baitfish in this area to hold fish.

FISHING A TEASER RIG

If you're fishing plugs along an open stretch of beach, it's always a good idea to attach a teaser rig to increase your chances of hooking up. A teaser could be any of a variety of artificials, such as a fly, Femlee Eel, Fin-S Fish, or small bucktail, attached via a dropper loop to your leader. The teaser represents a small baitfish such as a spearing, rainfish, sand eel, mullet, peanut bunker, or other silvery bait—all common forage for any of our larger predators. When it runs ahead of your plug, the setup simulates a larger fish chasing smaller bait.

You should rig your teaser from 2 to 4 feet above your plug and keep mental notes as to which distance produces the most strikes over time. Some days fish will hit the teaser when it's close to the plug; on other days they find the longer distance more enticing.

You'll catch a lot of fish on the teaser; on some days it will outproduce your plug. When bass or blues are blitzing it's not uncommon to get two fish at one time, known as a doubleheader. And sometimes when you're reeling in a catch that hit the plug, your teaser will get hit, too. Bluefish are notorious for this type of behavior.

Fishing a teaser rig is very effective technique for increasing your cast-to-catch ratios. It's a method I strongly encourage along any of New Jersey's beaches.

From 30th Street to 93rd Street you'll find a series of 14 groins that hold bass throughout the season. Captain Joe recommends fishing these groins from the beach; they're usually submerged at high tide. He suggests casting over the top of the rock piles with swimming plugs and poppers and allowing your offering to be swept into the downtide side of the rocks. A blue and white or red and white Gibbs popper is a local favorite. At 93rd Street you'll find a new jetty that's fishable at low tide. It's posted against fishing but frequently used.

At the southernmost end of the island is the Townsends Inlet, an unimproved inlet with no rock jetties. From the 93rd Street Jetty to the Townsends Inlet Bridge into Avalon is a 200-yard stretch of beach that's frequently fished. At the base of the bridge is a small parking lot. Along the beach under the bridge and around to the bay side you'll find some deep drop-offs. You can fish along this beach to the point where the condominiums begin.

A large sandbar runs down the center of the Townsends Inlet itself. This bar runs parallel to the north side of Avalon and will have plenty of breakers when the wind is up. The channel to navigate through the inlet runs between this bar and the north side of Avalon. It's approximately 1/4 mile wide and fairly deep—from 20 feet to 50 feet in spots. A small northeast cut that runs along the Townsends Inlet side is not recommended as a way out to the ocean; leave this route to the knowledgeable locals.

Captain Joe mentions that fishing the inlet by boat is far better in spring than fall. May and June are the best months; weakfish are the main targets at this time. Tiderunners of up to 10 pounds are frequently taken. The preferred method is bouncing off the bottom leadhead jigs tipped with 5 3/4-inch Fin-S Fish in all-white, Arkansas shiner, or the bright orange atomic chicken.

On the backside of Sea Isle City try Ludlam Bay in spring for small blues, and in summer for fluke. The north end of the bay is most productive from markers 337 through 346 in the Intracoastal Waterway. The channel here is from 9 to 11 feet deep. Work the drop-offs along the channel ledges.

On a changing tide Captain Joe points out that half the bay empties to the north, the other half to the south. This provides plenty of opportunities to find moving water that will give a favorable drift. Bucktails tipped with mackerel strips or squid will account for most of your fluke.

Other productive areas that Captain Joe mentions include Flat Creek, which runs north from the bay out to the Corson Inlet; from marker 337 north to the first creek mouth on the south bank—a favorite location on the outgoing tide; and Ludlam Thoroughfare at the southern end of the island. Captain Joe points out that nighttime in summer can be productive for the fly fisherman who casts up against the bank with black Deceivers or Seaducers.

Surf-fishing tournaments go on throughout the season all along our coast, but the one in Sea Isle City at the end of October is worth special mention. This tournament is hosted by the Women's Surf Fishing Club and open to all teams and individuals. Headquarters is at the Marine Recreation Center located at 42nd Street and the bay. This host club is unique in New Jersey in that it's composed of all women anglers. For that matter, it may be the only such club along the entire eastern seaboard.

I had the pleasure of speaking with past president Flo Pancoast, who recently completed her five-year term. Flo told me that the Women's Surf Fishing Club was founded in 1952 on Long Beach Island. Today there are approximately 25 members who are passionate about their surf fishing. Over the years some pretty impressive catches have been registered by members, including the 30-pound bass Flo herself caught in the Long Beach Island surf. Flo is a big advocate of catch-and-release fishing and crushes all her barbs to facilitate releasing her hooked bass.

Crushing barbs has always been a controversial issue among New Jersey anglers. Those who do it report no fewer fish being beached, and those who don't argue, "Why risk losing a big fish?" It comes down to personal preference and thinking. Crushing down the barbs or filing them off will, however, make it easier to release hooked fish. That point is tough to argue with. Extra care and consideration for the fish will need to be exercised with barbed hooks.

In Sea Isle City beach buggy access is permitted from September 15 to May 15. Permits can be obtained from the police department located at 233 JFK Boulevard weekdays from 9 A.M. to 4:30 P. M. Beach access points are located at 22nd, 75th, and 85th Streets.

To get to Sea Isle City, take the Garden State Parkway to exit 17 to Sea Isle Boulevard. This will become John F. Kennedy Boulevard, and you're there.

STONE HARBOR

AVALON/EIGHTH STREET JETTY/HANDICAPPED
FISHING PIERS/80TH STREET MUNICIPAL
BULKHEAD/STONE HARBOR POINT

New Jersey's eighth barrier island is situated between the Townsends Inlet and the Hereford Inlet. This stretch of sand is 7 miles long and has been known as Seven Mile Beach since as far back as the early 1700s. At the northern end of this island is the borough of Avalon, which stretches from the Townsends Inlet to 80th Street. From 80th Street to 123rd Street lies the borough of Stone Harbor, which in turn ends at the Hereford Inlet. The island is bordered to the west by the Intracoastal Waterway and a maze of bays, sounds, channels, and thoroughfares.

One of the interesting topographic features of our coastline occurs at the northern tip of Avalon, which extends a mile farther into the ocean than does the land around it. As a result, an extensive sandbar is formed off this point, making for hazardous navigation in the Townsends Inlet whenever the surf kicks up. A north to south littoral current is responsible for depositing sand here. Because of this prominent change in topography the Avalon Chamber of Commerce promotes this quaint beachfront community as a vacation resort that is "cooler by a mile."

If you drive to the northernmost point of Avalon you'll come to the Townsends Inlet. Here you'll find the Eighth Street rock jetty and two smaller groins. This jetty is a good location for stripers and weakfish, which cruise the inlet throughout the season. There's a parking area here for approximately six cars, and more parking along the steel-girder seawall on Seventh Street.

Locals familiar with the inlet will drift the channel between the sandbar and the north side of Avalon. Fall is a prime time for drifting eels along the bottom of this channel. Another popular method here is casting plugs and jigs into the white water spilling over the bar. Many smaller-sized bass are taken in this manner.

Along the bay side of Avalon a number of handicapped-accessible piers and bulkheads provide access to some excellent fishing. These are located at 8th, 23rd, 33rd, 37th, Bay Park Marina on 54th, and 57th Streets. You'll also find a public launch ramp located in Bay Park Marina. The Avalon Sport Fishing Center, located between 15th and 16th Streets on the bay, is headquarters for a large fleet of charter and party boats.

Beach buggy access in Avalon is available from September 15 to May 15 for a permit fee of $10. Permits are obtained from the borough clerk or by writing for an application and enclosing a self-addressed stamped envelope.

At the southern end of the island is the borough of Stone Harbor. Incorporated in 1914, this seaside resort left a lasting impression on me as I traveled up and down the coast. There is a certain character about Stone Harbor that makes it distinctively different from many of our other beachfront communities.

One of the best locations to fish in Stone Harbor is the Hereford Inlet, at its southernmost end. This is an excellent spot: You can walk or drive around the point along the beach, and there's a large parking lot with plenty of parking.

Fishing along the inside of Stone Harbor Point will provide you with protection from the wind and waves when Mother Nature decides to show her powerful fury; just tuck behind the dunes and you'll be nicely sheltered. Casting small swimming plugs into the current can be very effective, but you need to pay attention to their action. As is the case anywhere along our coast, a plug that doesn't have the right action isn't going to entice any fish into striking.

FISHING A PLUG

Observe the way the plug is moving through the water. If it's spinning in a circle when you retrieve, you're most likely turning the reel handle too quickly. What you want is a side-to-side undulation as the plug moves through the water. In other words, it should wobble without turning over. If you're swimming your plug through a fast current, you may need to slow down your retrieve to the point where you're hardly turning the reel handle at all; the flow of the water over the plug will naturally cause it to move from side to side. If you're fishing a metal-lipped swimmer, you can also change its depth by slightly bending the lip either up or down.

Another consideration is the strong tidal currents produced in inlets; retrieving a plug through them can be tricky. You should cast your plug upcurrent of the tide and allow it to drift along naturally until it's directly across from you. From this point start a slow retrieve while the plug swings toward the beach. Continue your retrieve along the edges of the inlet. Don't rule out holding your plug stationary; it can sometimes stimulate violent strikes.

If taking the kids fishing is on your agenda in Stone Harbor, the municipal bulkhead that runs parallel to Great Channel on 80th Street is the place you want. This is another of those great spots along our coastline where the whole family can relax and soak up some sun while wetting a line. Snappers, weakfish, and an occasional bass or two can be hooked here.

In Stone Harbor beach buggy access is permitted from September 15 to June 15. The permit can be obtained from the office of the borough clerk at 9508 Second Avenue between August 15 and September 30 from 9 A.M. to 4 P.M., or by writing for an application and enclosing a stamped, self-addressed envelope. Beach access points are located at 85th, 96th, 102nd, 118th, 122nd, and 123rd Streets. Parking lots are available at 96th and 123rd Streets. Be aware that north of 122nd Street, you

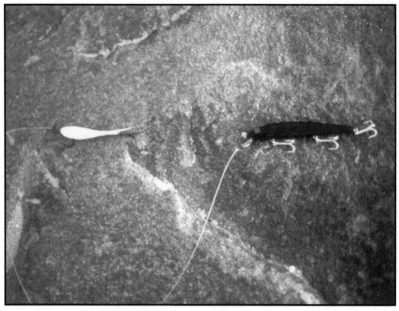

Use a plug and teaser combo to increase your chances of hooking up.
Jim Freda photo.

can operate a beach buggy from half an hour before sunrise until half an hour past sunset only.

To get to the municipal bulkhead in Stone Harbor take exit 10 off the Garden State Parkway and head east on Route 657, Stone Harbor Boulevard. Follow this to Third Avenue and make a left. From here go to 80th Street and turn left; you'll see the bulkhead access. On your way in you may want to stop at the Wetlands Institute, which is part of Rutgers University. It's on your right as you travel down the boulevard.

HEREFORD INLET
CHAMPAGNE ISLAND/MOORES INLET/
HEREFORD INLET PARK/NEW YORK AVENUE JETTY

At the southern end of the barrier island that's home to Avalon and Stone Harbor we come to Seven-Mile Point and the northern side of the Hereford Inlet. This inlet—approximately 7 miles south of the Townsends Inlet—is unimproved and bordered on its southern side by the town of North Wildwood. It's uncharted due to the ever-changing shoals and sandbars that are either created or destroyed by the large breakers of northeast storms.

Across the mouth of the inlet it's approximately 2 miles from Stone Harbor Point to North Wildwood Point. As you move into the inlet, the distance narrows to less than a mile. Over the centuries Mother Nature has opened and closed many natural inlets along the New Jersey coast, including Hereford. During the March 1962 nor'easter this inlet was washed over and closed. A shoal existed that allowed you to walk from one side of the inlet to the other. This was short lived, however; Mother Nature took back what she'd given with another storm.

Today these shoals constantly shift and change. They extend as far out as a mile offshore. Inside the inlet a sandbar—usually visible at low tide—is known to the locals as "Champagne Island." This bar can be as long as 1/4 mile and as wide as 100 yards.

The ever-changing sands of Hereford Inlet make it extremely hazardous to navigate the two narrow channels leading to its mouth, which thus isn't recommended as a way out to the ocean. It is, however, a location where both boaters and shorebound fishermen can find some of the best fishing the Jersey coast has to offer. The moving rips and shallow flats associated with these shoals produce a maze of favorable locations where predators can trap and ambush bait.

With a boat it's much safer to access the inlet from the backside, using the thoroughfares that lead out from Grassy

Sound behind North Wildwood or the Great Channel thorough-fares behind Stone Harbor. From either of these two points you can drift the channels without getting to close to the inlet mouth and near the zone of the breakers. At present Stone Harbor Channel is narrower than the channel on the Wildwood side. Both run directly along the shoreline on each side of the inlet.

These channels are excellent locations for stripers, blues, weakfish, fluke, kingfish, and red drum. Most locals will drift through these channels using 1/4- to 3/8-ounce bucktails tipped with white or pink Twister Tails for weakfish, or fish rubber shads or soft-bodied baits for bass. This is usually light-tackle fishing with 10-pound test. In fall, when the mullet and peanut bunker arrive, the preferred method switches to live baits.

If you decide to fish from shore the inlet can be accessed on foot from either side. On the Stone Harbor side you can trav-el down Second Avenue to 123rd Street and make a left. This will bring you into the municipal parking lot at Stone Harbor Point. You can park and walk the sand path to the inlet that's on your left. The other option is to obtain a beach buggy permit from the borough clerk's office and drive to the beach from this point. Due to the shoaling of sand that has occurred at Stone Harbor Point you'll be able to ride around the point to the inlet at low tide. You can continue to ride along the backside sandy beach for several hundred yards. It's convenient to wade these beaches while fish-ing the channel.

From the North Wildwood side you can access the inlet at the end of Central Avenue. This will bring you to the Moores Inlet parking lot, where you'll see the popular Moores Bar and Restaurant and parking for about 40 cars. You can also access the inlet from Hereford Inlet Park at the end of Surf Avenue.

When you pull into the Moores Inlet parking lot you'll see a fishing pier that has become obsolete. This pier was built at the water's edge, but because of sand deposition in front of it the pier now sits too far back from the water to fish from. You will also find a rock seawall here that curves and stretches for about

1/3 mile along the inlet's channel. This seawall, known as the New York Avenue Jetty, is the premier fishing spot in North Wildwood. The flat-topped seawall is easy to walk on and to fish from. Its close proximity to the channel draws in bait and predators throughout the entire season. This location is very popular in summertime; a lot of kids with the help of their dads get their introduction to our great sport here.

The seawall's point is in turn the most popular location along its entire length. Directly in front of the point the water drops to 25 feet. This spot is well known to locals for producing some rather large blackfish. Average-sized togs taken here are in the 3- to 5-pound range, with 7- to 10-pounders not uncommon. You'll even find a couple of fish each season that tip the scales at around 15 pounds. The channel along the seawall has an average depth of 15 to 20 feet and extends for 1/8 mile; it's 30 yards wide.

Swirling eddies and currents set up directly in front of the point. In fall, as the bait moves out of the back bay, it follows this channel along the seawall to get out to the ocean. This will be particularly true at low tide when the shoals across the mouth of the inlet block the bait from moving over the bar. Stripers, weakfish, and bluefish all ambush the bait as it gets confused in the swirling currents here. When the bite is on the area can get crowded, but it's well worth your time to find a spot along the seawall. Many vacationers will watch in amazement as fish erupt through schools of bait and an all-out blitz takes place only a few feet from the water's edge.

As you move down the inlet closer to its mouth, you'll come to Hereford Inlet Park. For the last five years a salt pond has been established along this North Wildwood beach, and the locals come here to net their bait in fall. Mullet and peanut bunker get trapped in this salt pond as the tide recedes, leading to what's known as "mullet mania." Anglers throw their nets and load up with baits. It's easy, convenient, and quick.

In the evening the local sharpies will fish this pond for weakfish, which either move into the pond or get trapped as the tide recedes. Here the method is similar to fishing a freshwater lake: It's bobber and worm time. Since the pond is void of any currents, floating bloodworms beneath a bobber is very effective. The weakfish are sitting ducks in this situation, and baits are eagerly accepted. Conditions, tides, and water levels in the pond have to be right for the weakies to set up like this, so a watchful eye is key.

GRASSY SOUND

STONE HARBOR FREE BRIDGE/NUMMY ISLAND /OCEAN DRIVE BRIDGE/NEW BRIDGE/BUOY 442 /OLD TRAIN BRIDGE/BUOY 454/RIO GRANDE BRIDGE

Nestled behind the Wildwoods is an array of channels, thoroughfares, creeks, flats, sounds, and islands representative of the type of waterways in southern New Jersey. These interwoven systems provide the angler with a refuge from the pounding surf and offer a tranquil setting for some relaxing fishing. You can appreciate the coastal beauty our state has to offer while viewing the setting sun from a front-row seat.

Behind the northern section of the Wildwoods are Grassy Sound Channel and Grassy Sound, both highly productive for stripers, weakfish, small blues, and fluke throughout their respective seasons. I had the pleasure of talking with Bill Donovan when researching the Grassy Sound area. Bill has fished these waters his entire life and is well recognized on the water. The managing editor of *New Jersey Angler Magazine*, Bill is thoroughly familiar with all of Grassy's nooks and crannies and pointed out to me some of the best locations to target here.

Grassy Sound Channel is a part of the Intracoastal Waterway that laces its way from the Hereford Inlet to Cape May Harbor. When you're fishing the extensive channels and thoroughfares behind the Wildwoods, Bill notes, there's a 4-mile stretch of waterway through the Intracoastal that's worth investigating. This area begins at the Stone Harbor Free Bridge that crosses Great Channel and ends to the south at the Rio Grande Boulevard Bridge, behind the center of Wildwood. The deepest water within this stretch is found within the channel of the Intracoastal Waterway. The majority of the area around Grassy Sound itself is only about a foot deep at low tide.

As in other parts of the state, the fishery here begins in early April when the water temperature approaches 50 degrees. The first fish to become active again after the winter season are small striped bass. Most of the fish caught will be slot fish but an occasional keeper is usually mixed in. Bill recommends using 1/4- to 1/2-ounce bucktail jigs tipped with a 4-inch white Twister Tail or 4-inch Fin-S Fish in natural colors. Lighter bucktails and jigheads are necessary due to the shallowness of the water you'll be fishing.

As mid-May rolls around, the Grassy Sound area really shines with its great weakfish run. Fish in the 7- to 9-pound range can regularly be caught, and some up to 10 pounds are taken each year. The daytime bite is mostly on Fin-S Fish, with a shift to bucktails after dark. By the end of May an excellent fluke fishery also develops in the area and extends into July. Many locals use a squid and mackerel strip combo on a simple single-hook fluke rig, with good results. A close second choice is a white bucktail tipped with a squid strip. In the early part of June anglers take a fair number of 5- to 7-pound fish. Small 1- to 2-pound blues also invade the area at this time.

As we come to the end of July this action starts to drop off, but the weakfish action picks up again. Average fish at this time are in the 3- to 4-pound range. The weakfish that you can consistently catch in the Grassy Sound area in summer are considerably larger than those in the rest of the state. Bill points out that one out of every five fish is in the 5- to 7-pound range. The best bite is right at first light and the first two hours thereafter.

When you're targeting these summer weakies Bill recommends concentrating on the downtide edges of the tidal flats; too many anglers spend too much time drifting the deeper holes and miss most of the action as a result. A second area to concentrate your effort is at the mouth of any of the creeks that empty into Grassy Channel. The action here is exceptional during low-light conditions and through the night.

In fall the Grassy Sound area continues to offer good weakfishing throughout September and into October. You'll also see the fall striped bass run beginning in late September, with an increase in the number of small- and medium-sized fish. This improves through October and November, with bigger fish available as the season wears on. Good fishing often lasts right through December and even into January if the weather isn't too extreme. Bill mentions that the two best bridges to work at this time are the ones around the Hereford Inlet: the Stone Harbor Free Bridge and the Ocean Drive Bridge.

Indeed, you'll want to spend a good deal of time working the waters around the Stone Harbor Free Bridge. This bridge spans Great Channel and connects to Nummy Island. A very deep channel that runs close to Nummy Island drops off to approximately 30 feet. On the Stone Harbor side of the bridge the water is much shallower, because of the presence of a sandbar. A favorite pastime for many boaters is to drift live eels under this bridge for stripers or to cast heavy bucktails.

On the Nummy Island side of the bridge you can pull off to the side of the road and park, then walk the sod banks east and west along the island. Try walking west for approximately 200 yards to the first creek mouth and fishing directly in front of it. Bill mentions this entire stretch as being very productive—this creek mouth in particular. You can fish on foot or from a boat.

East of the bridge you can walk 1/4 mile or so around the point into Dung Thoroughfare. Here you'll find water depths in the 5- to 10-foot range. At the mouth of the thoroughfare is a deep hole that drops off to 30 feet. Definitely fish this hole. Bill points out that the Stone Harbor Free Bridge is lit at night and produces shadow lines on the water, which large bass and weakfish use to their advantage as they lie in wait for unsuspecting prey. Work them over thoroughly.

As you move west (many would consider it south) from the Stone Harbor Bridge you'll come to the Ocean Drive Bridge, which connects Nummy Island to North Wildwood. Bill points out that there is extremely deep water toward the Nummy Island side of the bridge. These drop-offs can be reached from shore with spinning or conventional gear. If you're not in a boat, you can park on the Nummy Island side of this bridge and walk along the sod banks to access this water. You'll need to be careful, however, because the water drops off very quickly in front of you to about 20 feet. In the middle of the channel you'll find water in the 60-foot range. There's no parking on the North Wildwood side of the bridge. This bridge is also lit at night.

As you continue south along the Intracoastal Waterway you'll reach the New Bridge on North Wildwood Boulevard. Just before this bridge Bill points out that the 200-yard stretch of sod bank from Turtle Gut south to the "no wake zone" by the first house is very productive. The water here drops off to 20 feet. Stripers and weakfish move right up along these banks to get out of the swift currents here. This area is not accessible on foot; fish from your boat.

There's good structure around the New Bridge, with water depths in the 30-foot range. Either side of this bridge is a popular spot for anglers to drift for fluke in summertime. The concrete bridge pilings are very substantial, and bass and weakfish can be taken on their downeddy sides. Here you'll also see the old Route 147 Bridge; it was left half intact, and is now a public fishing pier offering access to some nice holes below. This is a very popular location throughout the season.

As you move south 100 yards from the New Bridge you'll come to Turtle Creek. Bill mentions that this creek is also a great spot for striped bass and weakfish. At its mouth, a large rip will develop during an outgoing tide. The creek depth is about 12 feet; you can run the creek with your boat for about 3/4 mile. As you navigate back in this water, the key is to look for other smaller creek mouths that empty into it. Fish these points.

Continuing south along the Intracoastal Waterway, Bill notes that the whole sod bank along Buoy 442 is worth investigating. Be conscious of nesting birds at this point, however: This bank is full of nesting terns and gulls from May to July, and they are very protective of their nests. Keep your distance. Across from this buoy you'll notice a giant tidal flat, which is productive on an outgoing tide—particularly if there's an east wind pushing water off this flat.

Moving south from here you'll reach the Old Train Bridge, with good fishing around the pilings that remain. Look for action on the upcurrent side of the pilings, especially on an incoming tide. Just south of this is Buoy 454, another excellent weakfish location. From here southward the channel isn't very pronounced, so it's best to work your way right to the next

A Grassy Sound Channel is a great weakfish hot spot in the late spring. Bill Donovan lands another beauty. Bill Donovan photo.

bridge: the Rio Grande Bridge, located directly behind the center of Wildwood. Here you'll find a popular location for fluke fishermen in summer. Water depths around the bridge are in the 25-foot range. If you're on foot, there's some shoreline access and parking on the western side of the bridge. No fishing is allowed from this bridge or any of the other bridges mentioned.

To get to the old bridge fishing pier, leave the Garden State Parkway at exit 6 and take Route 147 East. Go over the Grassy Sound New Bridge and make a left onto Ocean Drive. Take your first left onto the no-outlet road, and you're there. To access the area by boat, the Fifth Street Marina in North Wildwood is the most popular place to launch.

THE WILDWOODS
NORTH WILDWOOD/WILDWOOD/
WILDWOOD CREST

The ninth barrier island along the New Jersey coast is where you'll find the Wildwoods. This 7-mile stretch of beach is bordered to the north by the Hereford Inlet and to the south by the Cape May Inlet. The Wildwoods—which is comprised of three municipalities, the city of North Wildwood, city of Wildwood, and city of Wildwood Crest—is one of the largest free beach areas in the state. This area is often referred to as "Wildwoods' Five Mile Island."

I had the extreme pleasure of fishing with Jim Mooers from Rod Racks Unlimited when I visited the Wildwoods. Jim is well known in these parts as a veteran surfster and one of the top local experts when it comes to hooking fish. He's hardcore: He has a burning desire to have his feet in the sand and a rod in his hand. Jim also helped provide the information for the Hereford Inlet.

The beach topography of the Wildwoods is typical of southern New Jersey: a shallow shelf without any quick drop-offs between the beach and deeper water. Atypical of this area is that there are no jetties along the beachfront in this stretch of barrier island. The only jetties here are at the Hereford and Cape May Inlets.

As you look out into the water, you'll see an inner gully –bar–outer gully–outer bar. This formation changes regularly, however, due to the strong storms that batter the shoreline. Since the littoral current is flowing from north to south along the Wildwoods, you'll also notice the beaches growing wider each year at the expense of the neighboring Cape May beaches. The Cape May Jetty at the end of the Wildwoods blocks the free transfer of sand along the beach.

You'll do well on the Wildwoods beaches at high tide: The water along the inner gully will put fish right at your feet. During low-tide periods there are areas where you can wade out to the first bar and reach the drop-offs of the outer bar.

North Wildwood was founded in the 1890s as the tiny fishing village of Anglesea. Today surf fishing still reigns supreme as healthy numbers of surf anglers replace the summer crowds when fall arrives. Good beach buggy access is found along this entire stretch from September 15 to the Thursday before Memorial Day. There's a permit fee of $5 for North Wildwood residents and $15 for nonresidents. Permits can be obtained at the North Wildwood Police Station at 10th and Atlantic Avenue. Beach access points can be found at 5th and 15th Avenues.

The North Wildwood area is also home to the largest number of surf-fishing tournaments in the state in fall: There are five contests in which to compete for prizes, awards, and bragging rights. All occur in October: the New Jersey Beach Buggy Association Surf Fishing Tournament, the Pennsauken Surf Fishing Club Tournament, the Annual Great Fall Classic Surf Fishing Tournament, the Salt Water Fly Fishing Expo and Tournament (all Wildwood beaches), and the South Jersey Surfcasting Fishing Club Tournament.

Wildwood, located in the middle of the Wildwoods' Five Mile Island, is best known for its beach and boardwalk. The world-famous 2.5-mile boardwalk offers amusement rides, specialty shops, eateries, theaters, and water parks. Fishing, however, doesn't take a back seat to all these special happenings. Good beach buggy access is also available from September 15 to the Thursday before Memorial Day. The permit costs $15 and can be obtained from the city clerk's office at 4400 New Jersey Avenue. The beach access point is Cresse Avenue.

Wildwood Crest is at the southern end of the Wildwoods' Five Mile Island. Here town houses, condominiums, and hotels border the beach. No beach buggy access is permitted, and if you're interested in fishing the Cape May Jetty you'll need to walk the 2-mile distance to its rocks.

BEACH BUGGYING

Every fall the NJBBA Surf Fishing Tournament is really a special event that attracts mobile sport fishermen from all across the state. During this tournament hundreds of decked-out SUVs and recreational vehicles traverse the shoreline in search of that trophy catch. Many of the vehicles sport some of Jim Mooers's custom rod rack designs, which are patented and becoming very popular across the state.

Becoming a member of the NJBBA is a worthy endeavor. The NJBBA is a nonprofit organization incorporated under Title 15 of the Revised Statutes of New Jersey in 1954. It's primary goal is to maintain beach access for public uses, including fishing, operating a mobile sport-fishing vehicle, walking, birding, and horseback riding. The association also participates in projects to help preserve and conserve the marine and coastal resources along our shoreline.

Mobile sport-fishing vehicles are very popular in New Jersey and offer an alternative to purchasing a boat. You can quickly move from place to place on the beach or keep up with the fish and bait as they move along. You'll need to follow several regulations when operating a MSFV on any New Jersey beach. The following 11 items are mandatory to have in your possession:

1. Fishing equipment (rod and reel) and tackle or bait for each person over the age of 12.
2. Tire pressure gauge.
3. Spare tire.
4. Workable jack plus a support board (3/4 inch by 12 inches by 12 inches minimum).
5. Tow chain or snatch line.
6. Shovel.
7. Flashlight.
8. Coast Guard or ICC fire extinguisher.
9. Auto first-aid kit.
10. Litter or trash bag.
11. Minimum of three-quarters of a tank of fuel.

Basic *MSFV* rules of the beach are:

• *Stay off the dunes and vegetation.*
• *Speed limit 10 miles per hour.*
• *Drivers yield to the right. If you're in the vehicle tracks near a dune line heading north and an oncoming vehicle is coming south, for instance, you must give way. You would move to the right, closer to the ocean.*
• *No alcoholic beverages permitted.*

For membership contact: New Jersey Beach Buggy Association, Inc., P.O. Box 511, Seaside Park, NJ 08752.

Running a fully rigged beach buggy along the beach is just as effective as a boat for bringing you to the fish. Vehicles like Michael Winegard's are a common sight throughout the season. Eric Weeks photo.

CAPE MAY INLET
COLD SPRING/TWO MILE BEACH

Approximately 7 miles south of the Hereford Inlet is the last improved inlet along our coast. The Cape May Inlet, formerly known as the Cold Spring Harbor Inlet, is one of the easier inlets to navigate. The two rock-walled jetties that grace its entrance set the boundary line between Wildwood Crest and the beaches of Cape May.

The locals who have hopped these jetty rocks all their lives still refer to this as the Cold Spring Jetty. Its name is derived from the neighboring town of Cold Spring, where a spring of "sparkling" water bubbles forth in a salt marsh. In the late 1800s this spring was an attraction and reputed to be famous for its cure-all and medicinal properties. Invalids and others would journey here annually for a taste or touch of its sweet waters.

In the early 1900s the 2-mile stretch known as Poverty Beach on the Cape May side of the inlet was popularized as an automobile speed course. Spectators would come from miles around to catch a glimpse of some of the newfangled machines that raced across the hard sands.

Today public use and access are quite different. On the south side of the inlet the U.S. Coast Guard has set up a base and has limited beach access to Coast Guard personnel only. The north side of the inlet, along with the adjacent Two Mile Beach, has been periodically opened and closed by the U.S. Fish and Wildlife Service. The entire area has been deemed a potential nesting site for endangered piping plovers. Public outcry has been loud and many user groups, such as the NJBBA and the Recreational Fishing Alliance, are fighting to maintain public access to these prime fishing grounds without harming the nesting birds. Having access to the Cold Spring Jetty is vitally important to the jetty fishermen in this area. Its rips, its holes, and the currents along its sides have made this location a top-producing spot for trophy fish.

The inlet can be fished by boat and is known for producing excellent catches of striped bass, weakfish, and blackfish. Access from Cape May Harbor is easy. From the Parkway Bridge to the mouth of the inlet is 2.3 miles. Many fishermen use the inlet to head out to the popular Cape May Rips to the south.

The middle of the inlet channel ranges from 20 to 30 feet deep. Right off the tip of the South Jetty a quick drop-off extends down to 102 feet, but the bottom comes back up very quickly around this small area. The North Jetty doesn't have a deep hole at its end, as is characteristic of many inlet jetties along the northern New Jersey coast. This is because north–south littoral currents transport sand along the beach. The inlet jetties stop the free flow of sand along the beach. As a result, the Wildwood beaches north of the inlet are wide and well built up, while the Cape May beaches to the south are eroding.

The inlet can get very busy in summer and on weekends when the fishing is hot. For this reason drifting the inlet is best reserved for midweek or the off season, when boat traffic is at a minimum. Many savvy anglers let their boats drift inside along the inlet's rocks, and then out around the tip.

Striped bass and weakfish are the main targets here. Bucktails tipped with curly tails work well during the day in fall and beyond into the latter part of the season. Drifting live eels is the preferred method at night.

In fall the inlet sees an excellent mullet run, and anglers fishing the rocks are put right in the middle of the action with fish literally at their feet. Later in the season there's also a fine showing of peanut bunker and spearing.

As the holiday seasons approach in December most anglers in our state start to turn their attention elsewhere. For many the cold weather has become a nuisance, or perhaps other pressing obligations take priority. In any event, the number of fishermen along our beaches thins to the point that just the diehards are left. Many anglers new to the sport are unaware that some of the best striper fishing of the season can be had in late December and early January. This is particularly true of the Wildwood and Cape May area.

Typical water temperatures at this time of year range from 45 to 48 degrees. This temperature is approaching the lower tolerance limit of striped bass and stimulates them to continue their migration southward. The majority of the fish migrating along the Cape May beaches are heading back to the Chesapeake or to wintering grounds off the Carolinas. A resident population also enters Delaware Bay.

Just how quickly the surf temperatures drop depends a lot on how often a cold northwest wind blows in these weeks. If the wind patterns are from the east or northeast the water temperatures won't drop as quickly and the fishing season will be extended well into January.

Since a large percentage of the bass are moving south, the Cape May area still holds plenty of fish long after the northern and central parts of the state are done. Big bass in the 20- and 30-pound range can be caught in the middle of the day by casting surface swimmers such as Bombers and Dannys or by using top-water plugs. It's common to see fish crashing the surface and swirling on top.

To get to the Cape May Jetty take exit 4B off the Garden State Parkway. Go over the George Ridding Bridge to Pacific Avenue and make a right. Go 2 miles to Raleigh Avenue and turn left. You can park at the end of the road. From here you'll access the beach by walking through the LaQuinta Del Mar Condominium access. When you get on the beach you will see a sign for the national wildlife refuge on your right. The Loran Tower will also be visible. From here it's a 2-mile walk to the jetty.

CAPE MAY AND CAPE MAY POINT

BEACHFRONT/POVERTY BEACH/CAPE MAY HARBOR/
CAPE MAY POINT STATE PARK/BUNKER GUN
EMPLACEMENT/SUNSET BEACH

At the southernmost end of the New Jersey coastline we come to the 10th and final barrier island: the town of Cape May, one of the most popular vacation resorts along the Jersey shore. Cape May's historical roots run deep; it's currently the nation's only entire city designated a national historic landmark. The well-preserved 19th-century Victorian motif offers visitors the largest selection of meticulously kept bed-and-breakfast inns anywhere in the state.

Known in the 1600s as Cape Island, the early Quaker settlers here established a prominent whaling community and industry. It's documented that such early citizens as Henry Hudson and William Penn were influential in its establishment. In the late 1800s two railroads, the Reading and West Jersey, sparked the tourism industry and established Cape Island as a seaside resort. Most historians also agree that at the same time the Underground Railroad provided a haven for runaway slaves traveling across Delaware Bay from slaveholding Delaware.

Today the town's elegant ambience attracts nearly 100,000 visitors on a summer weekend. Many come for the fine food and restaurants that line the boardwalk or a stroll along the beaches in search of the famous "Cape May diamonds," the tide-worn quartz pebbles that are abundant here.

But many come to this place for a shot at some world-class fishing. Cape May boasts more state-record fish than any other location in New Jersey. The state-record amberjack, barracuda, bluefish, cobia, spiny dogfish, fluke, king mackerel, Spanish mackerel, tiger shark, and northern stargazer were all caught off Cape May. Because of its southern location more different species of fish are also available than anywhere else in the state.

The Cape May beachfront has eight accessible jetties and puts the surf angler in good position to tangle with stripers, blues, and weakfish. The northernmost end of the beach is bordered by the Cold Spring Inlet; the southern end by Cape May Point. The inlet is inaccessible from the beach because this area is restricted to Coast Guard activities and personnel. The area around the inlet is known as Poverty Beach and is an active bunker firing range.

Due to the shallow topography of the seafloor you'll find relatively calmer surf in Cape May than farther north—but also a series of rips moving along the beach. These rips are good spots to drift baits, particularly when they're located close to the beach. You'll also notice that the littoral current in this part of the state moves from north to south along the beach. As a result, there's significant beach erosion here, particularly at Cape May's southern end. This is due to the fact the Cold Spring Inlet jetties block the free transfer of sand along the beach. The net result is wide beaches in the Wildwoods.

Many boaters take advantage of Cape May Harbor at the northern end of town. The harbor offers excellent shelter and serene waters for targeting all the species of fish mentioned in this text. Because of its relatively shallow depth—6 to 10 feet—its water warms quickly in early spring and draws in some of the first stripers and weakfish of the season. The harbor is also a favorite location for the summer angler looking to tangle with some nice-sized fluke.

There are three ways to navigate into the harbor. From the east you can enter from the ocean through the Cold Spring Inlet; from the north you can use the Intracoastal Waterway; and from the west you can enter from the Cape May Canal. The harbor extends for 2.3 miles from the Parkway Bridge to the mouth of the inlet.

A fishing trip to Cape May would not be complete without setting out on foot to fish Cape May Point. Originally known as Sea Grove, this is a classic example of the jetty jock's ultimate dream. Eight jetties wrap around Cape May Point and are easily accessible. These jetties are relatively close together, so you can quickly hop from one to the next. The beauty of fishing these jetties is their breathtaking setting coupled with their excellent fishing. The Cape May Lighthouse stands directly behind, beaming a watchful eye over its domain. A Kodak moment on one of these jetties holding a trophy weakfish with the lighthouse in the background is a prized possession.

The Cape May Lighthouse was built in 1859, and is the third known lighthouse to be built at Cape May Point. The first was built in 1823, the second in 1847. The 1823 lighthouse succumbed to beach erosion and fell into the ocean, while the 1847 lighthouse was replaced due to faulty construction. The existing light is 157 feet, 6 inches tall.

The point's jetties are best known for weakfish. In early May weakfish start to arrive around the point that tip the scales in the 10-pound range. These fish are spawners and moving into lower Delaware Bay. Night action is also very good here throughout the summer; many bass will be mixed in with the catch.

The close proximity of the Cape May Point jetties makes the area a fishing wonderland for surfsters and jetty jocks. Jim Freda Photo

At the northern side of the point you'll notice a bunker gun emplacement that was built in 1942. When initially constructed it stood on high ground 900 feet from the ocean. Today, due to erosion, it sits in the water. The bunker held four 155-millimeter Coast Guard artillery guns that protected the entrance to Delaware Bay. A sister bunker stands across the bay in Lewes, Delaware. This area, along with the lighthouse, was designated Cape May Point State Park in the 1960s.

On the southern side of the point is Sunset Beach, where you can see a rather haunting structure resting just off the beach: This is the remains of the sunken freighter *Atlantus*. It was built of concrete during World War I due to a steel shortage.

To get to Cape May Point State Park take the Garden State Parkway to its end and cross over the Cape May Bridge onto Lafayette Street. Continue to travel straight to the intersection and bear right onto Sunset Boulevard (County Route 606). Follow this to Lighthouse Avenue and make a left into the park. If you continue straight on Sunset Boulevard to its end, you'll reach Sunset Beach and the remains of the *Atlantus*. The point's jetties will be right out in front.

Cape May Rips
EPH SHOAL/PRISSY WICKS SHOAL/MIDDLE SHOAL/SOMER SHOAL/OVERFALLS SHOAL

If I were asked to pick the one location that offers the best fishing along the 128-mile coastline of New Jersey, I would be hard pressed not to give the Cape May Rips top consideration. While there are other areas—the Reach in Sandy Hook Bay, and the sedge banks in Barnegat Bay—that would get my vote at times, the rips offer consistent catches of big fish, and in big numbers, too. The striped bass is king here, and double-figure catches of fish in the 20-pound range are so common that they don't even turn heads. Instead it's the 30-, 40-, and even 50-pound bass caught with hook and line that give the rips their well-deserved reputation.

Cape May Rips are located at the mouth of Delaware Bay. It's here at Cape May Point that the mighty Delaware River meets the Atlantic Ocean as it empties into Delaware Bay. The history of Cape May actually begins here in the bay. The early Dutch explorer Cornelius Jacobsen Mey investigated the Delaware River on excursions that led him to two capes separated by 17 miles of water. The northern cape he named Cape Mey and its sister to the south in Delaware he named Cape Cornelius. These names were later changed to Cape May and Cape Henlopen (another Dutch mariner), respectively.

The Cape May Rips are unlike any other fishing environment you'll encounter along the Jersey coast. The placid, serene bay waters around the point offer a false sense of security—venture just a mile or two beyond the shoreline and you'll find a series of shoals lying in a 3-mile radius from the point. These shoals are areas of extremely shallow water nestled in the deeper waters of Cape May Channel. While the channel depths sound to 35 feet, these shoals record depths of 3 feet or less at low tide. As the mighty Delaware empties over these shoals, tremendous rips are formed. With the right conditions of wind against tide these shoals actually cause the water moving over them to swell up and produce waves. Waves that crest and break and can reach heights in excess of 10 feet. Waves that think nothing of taking a 30-foot vessel and capsizing it. One of the earliest explorers in this area, Henry Hudson, was one of the first navigators to document the hazards presented by the rips.

These same currents and water conditions lure and hold trophy stripers—and as a result trophy hunters. The small-boater should exercise extreme caution, however, because these vessels are no match for the rips' awesome power. A good knowledge of the bottom topography and exact location of each shoal is essential for personal safety. Still, despite the dangers, the Rips can be overcrowded when the peak of the run occurs toward the end of May and into the beginning of June. It's not uncommon to find several hundred boats here when the action heats up.

Five rips are the main targets of local sharpies and charter captains looking for big stripers. These rips are formed on the Eph Shoal, Prissy Wicks Shoal, Middle Shoal, Somer Shoal, and Overfalls Shoal. In my research into the area I was fortunate enough to have Captain Mark Hansen of the charter boat *Treemendous* out of Cape May provide me with firsthand experience and knowledge as we navigated and fished these shoals.

The most impressive statistic from Captain Mark was the average number of stripers that an experienced angler could take per trip at the peak of the season: 20 to 25 fish, with the average striper weighing 25 pounds. And it isn't uncommon to have stripers in the 30- to 40-pound range mixed in. You'd be hard pressed to find such numbers anywhere else in the state.

The peak season for trophy stripers is spring, when the large spawning population enters through Delaware Bay on their way up the Delaware River. In particular, fish from the third week in May until the second week in June. This will vary somewhat each year depending on the water temperature, which acts as a stimulus to the spawn. The local sharpies fish the rips mainly at night during this period to produce trophy bass and to avoid the boat traffic. If you don't have a thorough knowledge of these waters I don't recommend this.

In early April you'll find less boat traffic to contend with at the Rips. Big fish can also be had at this time early in the season. By the middle of June the bay waters have warmed considerably, and the stripers are out of their comfort zone. Action comes to an end and doesn't pick up again until the water cools in late fall. When late October rolls around, the second so-called trophy season opens on the rips as 55-degree water temperatures usher in prime-time fishing. Fish in the 30-pound range are caught, though not with the consistency you see in spring. Still, impressive numbers and poundage are brought on deck.

Anglers drifting live eels through the Rips traditionally take the largest bass. The best action is at night but, again, leave this for guys like Captain Mark and the locals. The Rips should be fished during the daytime for the inexperienced. Captain Mark's recommended live-eel rig consist of 30-pound braid as a main running line connected to a 4-foot leader of 50-pound test. A 4/0 or 5/0 hook and 2-ounce in-line sinker round out the setup. Hook the eel under the chin and out the eye socket to ensure that a bass can't pull it from the hook without swallowing it.

Another method that consistently produces fish is bucktail jigging. Bucktails in the 1/2- to 2-ounce range in white or yellow are very effective. Tip these jigs with either mackerel or herring strips, or use a plastic Curly Tail Worm for best results. Fin-S Fish and Sassy Shad jigs also take a good number of bass. All of these baits will be chomped on, however, when the bluefish arrive—usually after the water hits about 58 degrees. Other artificial baits that work well are metals such as a Hopkins or crippled herring. Bomber-style plugs or Yozuris are also effective.

Presentation of your baits is important. They should travel naturally over the rips and as close to the bottom as possible. A bait drifting high in the water column isn't as effective. This is not to say that surface blitzes don't occur—they do, and they can be quite a sight.

There are two ways to get out beyond Cape May Point to the Rips. Starting at Cape May Harbor, the easiest course is through the Cape May Canal. This canal is approximately 2 miles long and will bring you to Delaware Bay on the western side of the point. As you near the canal's end you'll see the terminal for the Cape May–Lewes Ferry on your right. Small-boaters should exercise caution when the ferry is in the canal; always yield right-of-way. Upon entering the bay you'll be in Bay Shore Channel. Head due south as you make your way past the concrete shipwreck of the *Atlantus*. The moving rip of Eph Shoal will become visible. This is the closet rip to the beach. If you continue from Bay Shore Channel into Cape May Channel, you'll run adjacent to Prissy Wick Shoal. The other shoals are west from here.

The second way to access the rips is from the Cold Spring Inlet at the northern end of Cape May. This is a longer route—approximately 5.2 miles from the inlet to the rips. You'll be running along the outer beaches in the ocean, so the going can be somewhat rougher than in the canal. Either way, though, get yourself to the Cape May Rips. You will not be disappointed.

The Cape May Rips deserve top consideration as one of the best spots along the entire New Jersey coast for trophy bass. Jim Freda photo.

CONSERVATION

I hope you enjoyed this book and are able to use it not only as a guide for discovering some very productive locations throughout New Jersey but also a source of tips and techniques that benefit your own fishing experience. I've developed most of these tactics through countless hours on the water with either a fly or spinning rod in my hand. It never ceases to amaze me, however, that each time I step onto the sand or into a boat I do so with the same enthusiasm I had as a youngster. I crave that moment when the strike occurs and my rod pretzels over. As the battle ensues I am for a brief period of time in a world of my own. Eventually my quarry comes to rest at my feet and a quick photo captures the memory for a lifetime. The valiant fighter is then released as I give back what I have taken.

All the species we target have survived for centuries under Mother Nature's cyclical laws. The fate of New Jersey's abundant but delicate fisheries now rests with each of us, however. We must each do our part to conserve and protect our resources for future generations to enjoy.

I personally advocate catch-and-release but hold no contention against any angler who wants to bring home a meal for dinner. Bag limit and fisheries management laws are in place with good intentions to protect the species. Not all anglers may agree with them, but they must still abide by them.

Let your voice be heard if you feel strongly one way or the other on these issues. Write your legislators or congressmen. Join a fishing club or one of the many politically active recreational conservation groups such as the Jersey Coast Anglers Association, Recreational Fishing Alliance, Coastal Conservation Association, or Association of Surf Angling Clubs. It's your right to act, but remember to act responsibly and conservatively. This will ensure that Mother Nature continues her illustrious work with minimal interference from us. Good fishin'!

BIBLIOGRAPHY

Images of America, Point Pleasant, compiled by Jerry A. Woolley (Arcadia Publishing, 1995).
The New Jersey Coast in Three Centuries, Vol. I, II, III, William Nelson, editor (
Lewis Publishing Company, 1902).
Six Miles at Sea: A Pictorial History of LBI, NJ, John Bailey Lloyd (Down the Shore Publishing and The SandPaper, Inc., copublishers, Box 353, Harvey Cedars, NJ 08008).
The New Jersey Shore, John T. Cunningham (Rutgers University Press, 1958).
Down the New Jersey Shore, Russell Roberts and Rich Youmans (Rutgers University Press, 1993).
A Cruising Guide to New Jersey Waters, Captain Donald Launer (Rutgers University Press, 1995).

FISHING REGULATIONS AND RESOURCES

The following Internet sources will provide the most current fishing regulations and information:

For saltwater minimum size, possession limits, and seasons:

Bureau of Marine Fisheries   http://www.state.nj.us/dep/fgw/marfhome.htm

For state records of marine sport fish

http://www.scottsbt.com/fishids/regsrecs/njsaltrec.htm

OTHER USEFUL RESOURCES

National Marine Fisheries Service   http://www.nmfs.noaa.gov

Atlantic States Marine Fisheries Commission   http://www.asmfc.org

Jersey Coast Anglers Association   http://www.jcaa.org

Recreational Fishing Alliance   http://www.savefish.com

Association of Surf Angling Clubs   http://www.asaconline.org

New Jersey Beach Buggy Association   http://www.njbba.org

New Jersey State Federation of Sportsmen's Clubs

http://www.njsfsc.org/njsfsc.index.html

International Game Fish Association   http://www.igfa.org

Clean Ocean Action   http://www.cleanoceanaction.org